LUFTWAFFE TRANSPORT UNITS

1943 1945

'The last Ju 52s taking part in the Berlin just landed with their troops still aboard. The air movement controller believed that the previous night was the last on which it would be possible to reach Berlin as aircraft were no longer able to land there. Over the city, very large columns of smoke were coming from innumerable fires, and orientation was almost impossible. A chain of extremely heavy defensive fire was positioned along the approach to the Axis, all airfields were closed, and it was no longer possible to reach the centre of Berlin, even from Gatow. The crews of the transport Junkers to whom I had spoken confirmed the picture.'

General der Flieger Karl Koller, Chief of the Luftwaffe Generalstab,
describing the situation at Rechlin airfield on 27 April 1945
during attempts to supply Berlin.

1943-1945

Air Transport in the Mediterranean November 1942 to May 1943

On 8 November 1942, the Allies launched Operation 'Torch' and landed British and American troops in Morocco and Algeria. The Allied plan was to destroy Axis positions in North Africa by advancing these forces from the east while General Bernard Montgomery's Eighth Army pursued *Feldmarschall* Erwin Rommel's forces from the west. However, although the landings themselves were successful, the Allies had miscalculated the likely enemy reaction. They believed that the Germans would have difficulty in transferring troops and equipment for sustained operations, so when the Germans immediately raced to establish and hold a bridgehead in Tunisia, their speed and determination far exceeded anything the Allies had expected.

Fighter, fighter-bomber and bomber units were immediately rushed to Tunisia, some of the latter arriving from as far afield as Norway. But the most impressive, indeed astonishing, of the *Luftwaffe's* achievements was the reinforcement of its air transport fleet. This was a necessary prerequisite as the sea routes to Tunisia were unsafe due to Allied superiority, yet troops and equipment had to be ferried in as rapidly as possible. German dependency on air transport in the theatre, already important, therefore increased, and the air transport force was eventually expanded from 205 to 673 aircraft.

RIGHT AND FAR RIGHT: A direct hit on an Axis cargo vessel and (far right) tracer converging on a merchantman. Throughout the long North African campaign, Axis sea routes were harassed by Allied aircraft and by the ships and submarines of the Royal Navy. In view of the enormous amount of valuable war materials lost at sea, the role of the *Luftwaffe's* Transporters was particularly important.

As early as 9 November, all air transport capacity was temporarily diverted from Rommel's forces, then retreating through Egypt towards the Libyan border, and by the end of that day, 3,000 additional troops had already arrived in Tunisia. By the 10th, these troops had established a bridgehead and defensive perimeter, while additional transport units were already being transferred from Russia as well as from bases and training schools in Germany. Moreover, the ground forces arriving were of the highest quality, and almost 11,000 troops which arrived within the first 14 days included crack *Panzer Grenadier* regiments and *Fallschirmjäger* accompanied by heavy equipment, armour and motor transport.

Among the first aircraft transferred to meet the situation caused by the 'Torch' landings were a number of six-engined Me 323 transports based at Athens-Eleusis in Greece. These large aircraft, each capable of carrying a load of up to 14 tons, belonged to I./KGzbV 323, which soon began supply sorties to Tunisia. Indeed, the first Me 323 lost in North Africa was from this *Gruppe* and was destroyed at Tunis-El Aouina on 10 November 1942 during a strafing attack by RAF Beaufighters.

In addition to the Me 323s, 167 Ju 52/3ms from Germany and Russia arrived in Italy and Sicily and were formed into composite *Gruppen* named KGrzbV 'Wittstock', KGrzbV 'Frankfurt', KGrzbV S.7, KGrzbV S.11 and KGrzbV S.13. The letter S in the latter designations indicated 'Schule', for these units were indeed largely created from aircraft and personnel from the training units and had only met their *Gruppenkommandeure* and *Staffelkapitäne* for the first time when they arrived in the assembly area. Although these crews were courageous and their morale was high, they naturally had no operational experience and therefore lacked nearly all the qualifications for their difficult task. It was for this reason that each *Gruppe* usually included one *Staffel* composed of experienced operational crews. No sooner had this additional transport force been arranged, however, than the situation in Russia demanded that some be withdrawn and by 26 November, 150 of these aircraft had already been recalled and re-assigned to *Luftflotte* 4 for the supply of Sixth Army at Stalingrad.

Meanwhile, air transport to Rommel's forces in Libya had been reinstated, but the retreat of his army was now so rapid that it was moving beyond the range of air supply from Crete and, after 20 November, all air supply sorties had to be flown from Italy and Sicily to Gabes and Castel Benito

ABOVE: German reaction to the Allied landing in Tunisia was immediate and relied on the Luftwaffe's air transport units to ensure the rapid transfer of reinforcements. Here a loose formation of Ju 52/3ms flies over the Mediterranean during a return flight from Tunisia to Sicily.

airfields, situated either side of the Tunisian-Libyan border. The Ju 52/3ms on this route often flew in formations of between 50 and 60 machines or more and relied on the well-tried tactic of opening concentrated defensive fire and reducing height to just above the sea. To some extent, this proved effective but as their route was now much closer to Allied bases, the *Transportverbände* suffered great losses caused by fighters or attacks on their airfields.

Some idea of the strain which the operation to supply Rommel's army imposed upon the aircrews involved may be gained from the experience of *Fw.* Hermann Rahm, a flight mechanic from *Transport Staffel/*II. *Fliegerkorps*. On 9 December, his aircraft took off from Castel Benito aerodrome in company with some 30 to 35 other Ju 52/3ms to return empty to Trapani. The formation flew at a height of about 30 metres and was escorted by two Bf 110s and two Ju 88s, but between the coast of Tunisia and the island of Lampedusa, it was attacked by RAF Beaufighters. Two or three Ju 52/3ms were shot down, one of which was Rahm's machine, which caught fire and crashed into the sea. Only Rahm and the pilot survived and were rescued two days later by a British submarine. Since arriving in the Mediterranean, the *Staffel* had worked hard carrying aircraft spares, fuel and other supplies, so that when informed of the German retreat from El Agheila, the realisation that the entire supply effort had been in vain caused Rahm to break down in tears.

The German evacuation of El Agheila was completed on 16 December, and on 23 January 1943, the British Eighth Army occupied Tripoli, crossing into Tunisia on 4 February. *Transporter* aircraft supplying German forces in the north and east of the country now flew in a stream of approximately 100 aircraft broken down into smaller groups following one another at close intervals. The transport streams were originally escorted by a few Bf 109 or Bf 110 fighters, but as the Allied air forces established themselves and enemy fighter activity intensified, there were never enough fighters

ABOVE: Throughout the Tunisian campaign, the bulk of airborne supplies were conveyed in Ju 52/3ms operating from Naples or from Sicily and Reggio. In both cases, the aircraft rendezvoused off Trapani and made the last stage of their journey at low level. Apart from the machine from which the photograph was taken, 26 other Ju 52/3ms may be seen here, although formations usually consisted of some 50 or 60 aircraft.

RIGHT: A scene on a dusty airstrip in Tunisia showing the tail of an aircraft with the tactical rudder markings of 3./KGzbV 400. This particular machine is thought to have been a Ju 52/3mg4e, W.Nr. 5173, which had been drawn from Flugzeug-führerschule (C) 7 and carried the Stammkennzeichen DS+AF.

ABOVE: Air transport to Tunisia was organised by the Lufttransportführer Mittelmeer based in Rome, a post taken over in February 1943 by Generalmajor Ulrich Buchholz. Born in Landsberg on 22 December 1893, Buchholz fought in the First World War as a Leutnant with the Army and then flew with several units as an observer and pilot. He transferred to the Luftwaffe in 1935 and, in March 1940, after a number of different assignments, became Kommodore of KGzbV 3, a staff unit controlling various Transporter units and held this position until January 1943. He then became Lufttransportführer Mittelmeer until May 1943, in which month he was awarded the German Cross in Gold. He was subsequently appointed Transportführer 1, a position he held until the end of November 1944. He is shown here as a Generalleutnant in 1944 wearing the Royal Rumanian Order of the Star, with Swords. Generalleutnant a.D. Buchholz died in Mölln in June 1974.

available to increase the escort accordingly. Neither was there any let-up in fighter-bomber attacks on the unloading depots at Tunis-El Aouina and Bizerta. In a single attack on El Aouina on 18 January 1943, a total of 23 Ju 52/3ms was destroyed and a bombing raid on the 22nd completely destroyed a further 15 and damaged another 13.

Responsibility for air transport to Tunisia rested with the *Lufttransportführer Mittelmeer*, who maintained a large organisation in Rome. At the beginning of 1943, this post was occupied by *Oberst* Rudolf Starke, but in February he was replaced by *Generalmajor* Ulrich Buchholz, previously the *Kommodore* of KGzbV 3 in South Russia. One of *Generalmajor* Buchholz's first duties was to congratulate air-gunners aboard transport aircraft for their victories over Allied fighters. One was a rear gunner aboard a Ju 52/3m of KGzbV 'Frankfurt' which was coming in to land on the night of 12/13 February when it was attacked by a British night fighter. The gunner succeeded in shooting down the fighter while it was making its third attack. Another incident involved two Me 323s which were returning to Italy from Tunisia when they were attacked by P-38s, and two gunners of one of the Me 323s received special mention for having destroyed a US fighter.

Meanwhile, an Allied study of German air transport traffic patterns had revealed the importance of this role, and once this was realised, the Allies planned a determined campaign to strangle the air transport effort carrying supplies and personnel into Tunisia. Code-named 'Flax', the operation was directed against the large air transport convoys themselves and against the airfields they were using in Sicily and Tunisia. It began on 5 April and was first conducted by Allied aircraft operating from bases in northern Tunisia and Algeria. On the first day, an escorted formation of 31 Ju 52/3ms was intercepted by P-38s which shot down 14 transports plus several escort fighters. Further losses were inflicted on the transports on the 10th and 11th, and on the 17th the operation was taken over by fighters of the Western Desert Air Force operating from bases between Akarit and Enfidaville. These were responsible for the heaviest loss of the operation, which occurred off Cape Bon at approximately 1800 hours on the 18th when P-40s intercepted an escorted formation of 68 Ju 52/3ms. The transports, returning to Sicily with German and Italian service personnel, were flying low over the sea in three Vee formations covered by Bf 109s, MC 202s and Bf 110s, and in the resulting battle, the *Luftwaffe* lost ten fighters and 33 Ju 52/3ms shot down plus another nine Ju 52/3ms damaged.

Four days later, on 22 April 1943, some 20 Me 323s of I. and II./KGzbV 323 were flying in a loose formation just above the sea when they were attacked near Zembra Island off the Tunisian coast by P-40s of the SAAF. In the ensuing battle, six aircraft from I./KGzbV 323 and eight from II. *Gruppe* were shot down into the sea, and of the 140 German flying personnel involved, only 19 were saved. Among those who died was *Obstlt*. Werner Stephan, the *Kommandeur* of II./KGzbV 323, who was travelling in one of the aircraft as a passenger. Total

personnel losses between 18 and 24 April alone amounted to some 320 men, and in the same period, 240 tons of supplies, 14 Me 323s and more than 50 Ju 52/3ms were also lost due to all causes.

Total *Transporter* losses directly attributable to Operation 'Flax' are difficult to establish, but from 5 to 24 April appear to be 14 Me 323s, four SM.82s and 123 Ju 52/3ms. When other losses due to Allied bombing and accidents are taken into consideration, the total may have been as high as 157 transport aircraft. On the 25th, and as a direct result of these heavy losses, *Reichsmarschall* Göring ordered that all transport flights to Tunisia were to be undertaken only at night. This brought Operation 'Flax' to an end but also reduced the scale of Axis air deliveries so that even Ju 88s were called in to drop supplies.

When the end of the battle for Tunisia was clearly in sight, part of the staff of *Fliegerführer* Tunis and certain operational units were flown out to Sicily and Sardinia. In the first week of May, a last-minute attempt was made to evacuate wounded and other *Luftwaffe* units from Bizerta and Cape Bon by transport aircraft arriving with ammunition. In order to ensure a maximum number of sorties, crews were required to fly daily, and with little rest between flights. This placed them under severe additional strain, but with a great number of people awaiting transport, they nevertheless continued to fly, often

LEFT:
Photographed
between Sicily and
Tunisia in May
1943, a formation
of Ju 52/3ms
comes under attack
by USAAF B-25s
and P-38s. Only
part of the low-
flying formation,
believed to have
consisted of
35 Ju 52/3ms,
is visible here.

with their aircraft dangerously overloaded. The last transport flight to Tunisia was made on the night of 12 May, and on the same day, resistance in the last Axis-held area in Tunisia collapsed and German and Italian troops laid down their arms. The following day, the Allies attacked the few remaining defences and, lacking fuel and ammunition, the Axis forces in Tunisia surrendered.

Transporter losses in Tunisia between 8 November 1942, when the Allies mounted the 'Torch' landings, until the capitulation on 12 May 1943, were very heavy and it is thought that more than 350 transport aircraft were destroyed [1]. Whatever the true figure, the effect of these losses, together with those experienced in Russia during the winter of 1942/1943, were sufficient to cripple the *Luftwaffe's* transport arm for the rest of the war.

BELOW: According to Luftflotte 2's war diary, in January 1943 the Transporters flew a total of 15,415 personnel, 4,728 tons of arms, instruments and ammunition, 149 tons of fuel and 8.5 tons of food to Tunisia.

1. In Volume II of 'The Royal Air Force 1939-1945', by D. Richards and H. Saunders, the number of Transporter losses is given as 432. This, however, was an estimate, probably based on inflated Allied claims.

1943-1945

ABOVE AND INSET: Of the loads carried by aircraft departing from Tunis, evacuated Italian soldiers and civilians formed a high proportion, with aircraft engines, tank engines, olive oil, wounded and prisoners of war accounting for much of the remaining cargoes. At least 5,600 prisoners of war were evacuated by air during the four months from December 1942 to March 1943 and departures were particularly heavy between 19 February and 2 March, when 3,500 PoWs were evacuated. Here, Italian soldiers and Commonwealth PoWs (*INSET*) are seen waiting to board an Me 323.

RIGHT: A BMW 132 radial engine being unloaded from a Ju 52/3m after being flown out of Tunisia.

LEFT: An Me 323 D-6, still carrying its Stammkennzeichen RF+XD on the fuselage sides. This aircraft, W.Nr. 1130, is known to have operated with I./KGzbV 323 in Sicily and Tunisia between March and May 1943. The normal load of these aircraft when flying to Tunisia was 12 tons, which required a take-off run of about 1,000 metres. Very occasionally, the aircraft took off with a load of 14 tons, apparently without difficulty, but landings were not without hazard. In Tunisia, Ju 52/3ms in the landing pattern had to give Me 323s priority, but even in the best of circumstances, the pilot of a fully laden aircraft had to make a perfect landing if damage to the undercarriage was to be avoided.

ABOVE: Luftwaffe losses in Tunisia increased from February 1943 as the Allied air forces established themselves on forward airfields and subjected Luftwaffe bases to heavy bombing. Shown here are Ju 52/3ms with a large white W on their rudders indicating that they belonged to KGzbV 'Wittstock'. This unit consisted of a Stab and four Staffeln comprising aircraft from KGrzbV 9, KGrzbV 102, KGrzbV 106 and KGrzbV 700, all with their appropriate operational markings, plus aircraft from KGrzbV 300 with factory markings. KGzbV 'Wittstock', together with KGzbV 'Frankfurt', remained in the Mediterranean until March 1943 when both were withdrawn and their remaining aircraft were taken over by KGrzbV 106.

RIGHT: In March 1943, after suffering up to 60 per cent losses in Russia, I./KGzbV 172 was sent to Ludwigslust where it was re-equipped. While some personnel were sent on leave, the remaining crews were engaged in transporting troops of the 'Herman Göring' Division from Bordeaux to Tunisia via Italy. This photograph was probably taken at that time.

ABOVE: Although the weather in North Africa was generally good, men and machines alike were affected by the heat and dust. Personnel suffered from intestinal disorders while even special oil cooling devices and sand and dust filters for the aircraft could not entirely prevent engine breakdowns. Serviceability often decreased to some 50 per cent, and by the end of the fighting in Tunisia, some Staffeln possessed an average of only five serviceable aircraft. The red spinners and background to the badge on the nose of this aircraft, probably photographed in Sicily, identifies it as belonging to 10./KGzbV 1.

ABOVE: Open-air maintenance being carried out on a Ju 52/3mg7e. When the transport units were reorganised in May 1943, each Gruppe was allocated its own Flugbetriebskompanie or Aircraft Servicing Company, and although these were dissolved in January 1944, a workshop platoon was then allocated to the Gruppenstab and one Servicing Platoon was attached to each Staffel. Over the canopy on this machine is the Condor Haube in which was normally mounted an MG 15 machine gun. The badge on the nose is almost certainly that of KGrzbV 500.

RIGHT: The tactical code Z5, as shown on the rudder of the SM.82 in the background of this photograph, was reserved for the aircraft of the independent Savoia Staffel attached to KGzbV 1. Although 8., 10. and 13./KGzbV 1 are all known to have flown the SM.82, a Staffel, known simply as the Savoia Staffel, was attached to Stab IV/KGzbV 1 but never fully incorporated into the Geschwader's structure. Note the size and position of the swastika which, together with the yellow wingtips, are not typical of most other SM.82s operating with KGzbV 1.

LEFT AND RIGHT: An anti-aircraft gun being unloaded from an SM.82 of the Savoia Staffel of Stab IV./KGzbV 1 in North Africa. Note that this machine lacks the yellow wingtips shown previously and had a turret and astrodome over the cockpit area.

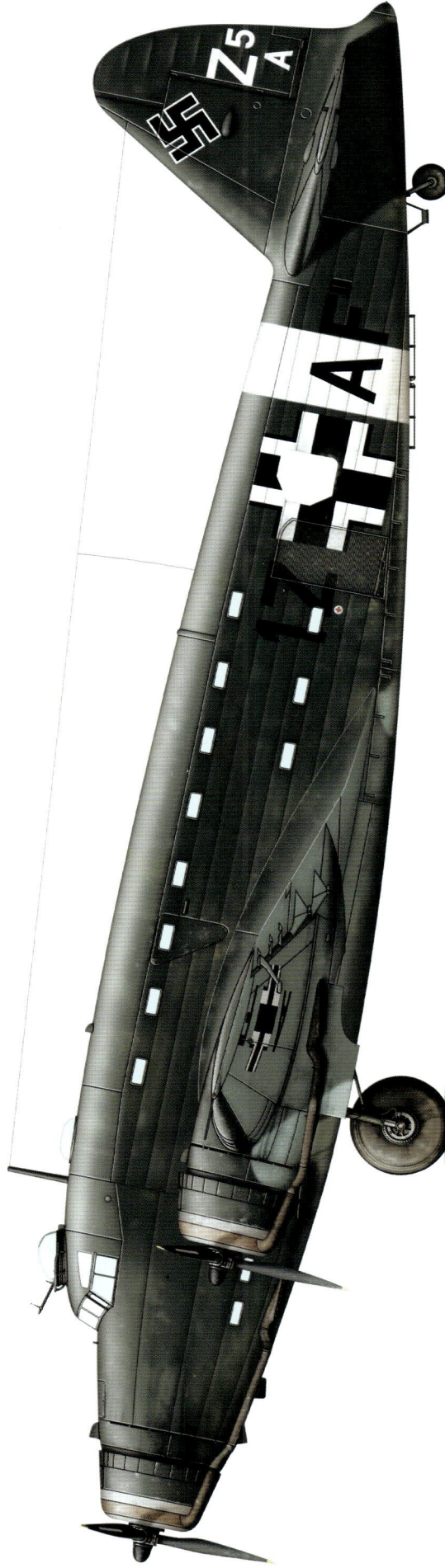

Savoia-Marchetti SM. 82 of the Savoia Staffel attached to Stab IV./KGzbV 1, North Africa, early 1943

This aircraft was coded IZ+AF and was finished in weathered Luftwaffe colours 71 and 65 with all national insignia correctly proportioned. A white band encircled the rear fuselage, and the propeller tips were yellow. The Staffel letter F on the fuselage is that of Stab IV./KGzbV 1 and the 5 in the white tactical code Z5A on the rudder indicates the fifth Staffel attached to the Gruppe.

1943-1945

ABOVE AND RIGHT: As with the Ju 52/3ms, the formations of Me 323s relied on their combined defensive fire and low altitude for protection. Nevertheless, the armament of the Me 323 was progressively increased as a result of Allied fighter opposition and some aircraft were fitted with 13 gun positions. Although the gunners lacked an intercom system, two warning horns were provided in the interior of the aircraft so that, by pressing an operating pushbutton provided by each gun position, any of the gunners could alert the rest of the crew to an attack.

LEFT AND ABOVE: After Rommel's retreat into Tunisia, the size of the transport formations increased to approximately 100 machines. While considerably fewer aircraft are visible in these mixed formations of SM.81s and Me 323s about to make landfall on the coast of Tunisia, they were almost certainly part of such a larger formation.

ABOVE: The winter of 1942/43 in Tunisia was the wettest in several years with heavy rainfall often affecting airfields. This photograph shows a light half-tracked vehicle of the SdKfz 250 series being unloaded from an Me 323, probably at El Aouina.

LEFT: Aircraft damaged in North Africa were frequently cannibalised to keep other machines flying before being consigned to the scrap heap. These discarded tail units are from aircraft of 1./KGzbV Frankfurt and 3./KGzbV 172.

RIGHT: A Piaggio P.108 T coded J4+JH of Transportgruppe 5. This unit was formed from LTSta. 290 in April 1943 and, in addition to the P.108, flew Ar 232, Fw 200, Ju 90, Ju 290 and Ju 252 aircraft.

1943-1945

ABOVE: The Ju 252 was designed and developed as a replacement for Lufthansa's Ju 52/3m, but only 15 examples were built and these saw limited service with the Luftwaffe. In April 1943, one of these machines, the Ju 252 V-5, W.Nr. 005, Stammkennzeichen DF+BQ, was assigned to LTSta. 290 and flew several sorties from Pomagliano to Tunis with mixed loads of some 4,000 kg in fuel and passengers. On one occasion, the load included a Kübelwagen, the same type of vehicle as shown in the background of this photograph. Later assigned the operational markings J4+LH, this aircraft was damaged in a landing accident on 24 April and destroyed a few days later.

LEFT: The letter N on the rudder of this aircraft indicates that it belonged to I./KGzbV 172 which reappeared in North Africa in April 1943 after re-equipping with replacement aircraft. These came from various sources, the badge on the nose of this example showing that it had been drawn from Stab/KGrzbV 105.

Nose detail showing the aircraft name and the badge of 1./KGzbV 172.

Shown towards the end of the fighting in Tunisia, this captured Ju 52/3m displays an interesting variety of markings. The code 4V was used by several units, but given the approximate date, i.e. before the end of the fighting in Tunisia in May 1943, the aircraft must have belonged to 1./KGzbV 172. The rudder, however, is a replacement which has evidently been removed from an aircraft belonging to 1./KGrzbV 800. Painted on the forward fuselage in white capital letters was the legend 'El Haouaria', a location on the rocky coastline of Cape Bon and evidently a place of some special significance to the crew. Note the incomplete roundel painted over the fuselage Balkenkreuz, suggesting that the RAF intended to repair and fly the machine.

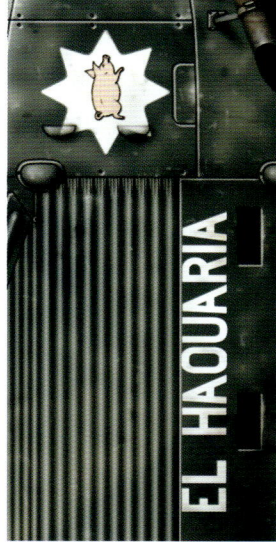

Junkers Ju 52/3m 4V+AT of 1./KGzbV 172, Tunisia, 1943

This aircraft was finished in the standard transport scheme of 70/71/65, although all top surfaces had been bleached by the sun to the extent that the demarcation between the colours was indistinguishable. The Werknummer 6518 appeared at the top of the fin and a white band encircled the rear fuselage. On the nose, in addition to the legend 'El Haouaria' in white, was the Staffel badge showing a pig superimposed on a white star. The replacement rudder was mottled in 79 and marked with the tactical code T1J in white. Note that this machine was fitted with a canopy designed for an MG mounting.

RIGHT: The Ju 290 was powered by four BMW 801 engines and could carry a normal load of between four to six tons. It had a crew of six and a maximum range of almost 6,500 kilometres. This particular example, a Ju 290 A-1 coded J4+AH, belonged to Transportstaffel 5, which had been formed from LTSta 290 in April 1943, and was photographed while being examined by US troops at Bizerta in Tunisia in May. When the Ju 290's hydraulically operated loading ramp was lowered, it raised the freight deck to the horizontal and allowed vehicles up to the size of a Kübelwagen to be driven straight into the aircraft's cargo hold.

RIGHT: This Ju 52/3m, photographed at Milo, near Trapani in Sicily, was almost certainly destroyed shortly before the end in Tunisia. The aircraft had belonged to 3./KGzbV 172 and carried the operational code 4V+JV with the individual aircraft letter on the fuselage in red, the Staffel colour, and the tactical code N3J on the rudder in yellow. In May 1943, after the end in Tunisia, the Transportverbände were reorganised and I./KGzbV 172 was reformed to create IV./TG 3.

LEFT: Although still wearing factory markings (?K+FQ), the tactical code T1G on the rudder of this machine, photographed after a bombing raid on Tunis-El Aouina, indicates that it had operated with 1./KGrzbV 800.

Ju 52/3m 8T+BK of 2./KGrzbV 800 at El Aouina, May 1943

The camouflage on this aircraft appeared relatively new, although slightly dusty, and some repainting was evident on the rudder where the tactical code had been changed. The overall camouflage was the standard 70/71/65 scheme and a white band had been painted around the fuselage between the first two characters of the unit code and the Balkenkreuz. The T in the tactical code T2B was consistent with that used by 2./KGrzbV 800, the 2 and the B representing the Staffel and the individual aircraft letter respectively.

1943-1945

ABOVE: The skeleton of a burned-out Me 323 on El Aouina airfield after the Axis surrender in Tunisia. Note the two-bladed propellers.

BELOW: This Ju 52/3m was captured in an airworthy condition in Tunisia by the RAF who repainted it with British markings but preserved the badge of IV./KGzbV 1 on the forward fuselage. The Ju 52/3m proved very popular with Allied air forces and several captured examples are known to have been repaired and made airworthy. Some machines repaired by the RAF were still flying at the end of the war.

The Reorganisation of the *Transportverbände*

Despite the fact that from 1940 to April 1943 the most important work of air transport had been re-supply, the transport units had remained under 7. *Fliegerdivision* and, later, XI. *Fliegerkorps*, which commands were mainly concerned with parachute and airborne operations. As a result of this arrangement, the transport units had been placed at the disposal and under the command of a multiplicity of staffs and there was no clear-cut chain of command and no single authority to supervise servicing, crew training and generally to maintain the units. In addition, but with the exception of KGzbV 1, the policy of constituting units only on paper and drawing them from training for special operations was still in force. The effects of these unsatisfactory arrangements had been felt during the whole of the winter of 1942/1943, but it was not until May 1943, once the air supply commitments to Sixth and Seventeenth Armies in Russia and to Libya and Tunisia in the Mediterranean were over, that the *Luftwaffe* was able to reorganise air transport to meet what had clearly developed into a long and defensive war.

Consequently, the *Kampfgeschwader zur besonderen Verwendung*, together with some regular *Kampfgruppen* which previously had been mainly engaged in supply work, were henceforth placed on a permanent footing, reorganised to form *Transportgeschwader* and redesignated, as shown over. These new *Transporter* units were placed under a newly created XIV. *Fliegerkorps* headed by *General der Flieger* Joachim Cöler who was thus responsible for all transport, communications and medical units, although at *Luftflotte* or *Fliegerkorps* level they were controlled operationally by a *Transportfliegerführer* or *Geschwaderstab*. The glider units remained subordinated to XI. *Fliegerkorps* and the *Luftlandegeschwader* retained their original designations.

The initial establishment for a Ju 52/3m *Transportgeschwader* was, at this time, 217 aircraft. Five of these aircraft were allocated to the *Geschwaderstab* and the rest were divided between four *Gruppen*, each with 48 aircraft in four *Staffeln*, plus a *Gruppenstab* with another five aircraft. As an enquiry into the Stalingrad airlift had revealed that large concentrations of transport aircraft resulted in technical difficulties, efforts were also made to improve servicing and each *Gruppe* was now allocated its own *Flugbetriebskompanie* or Aircraft Servicing Company.

Few changes were made to existing production plans, although manufacture of the old but well-tried Ju 52/3m was increased. As a result, production of the type peaked in 1943 when a total of 887 was produced. The sub-type manufactured in the greatest numbers was the Ju 52/3mg8e which had a loading hatch in the cabin roof as well as the standard doors in the fuselage sides. Apart from the transport version, some Ju 52/3ms were fitted with magnetic rings for minesweeping [2].

BELOW: An air-to-air view of a pair of minesweeping Ju 52/3ms, each fitted with a large degaussing ring.

LEFT: An analysis of the failure of the Stalingrad airlift revealed that apart from the loss of forward bases, a shortage of petrol and the poor weather, the concentration of as many as 300 aircraft on one airfield had resulted in maintenance difficulties. Anticipating that large numbers of transport units might again be required to be concentrated for particular operations, the reorganisation of the Transportflieger in May 1943 included technical facilities and each Gruppe was allocated its own Flugbetriebskompanie.

---

2. These aircraft were nicknamed 'Ehepaar', or 'Married Couples' as they always operated in pairs and because of the large hoop suspended beneath the wings and fuselage which was known as a 'Verlobungsring' or 'Engagement Ring'. The activities of these minesweeping units are, however, beyond the scope of this work.

1943-1945

The Creation of the *Transportgeschwader* and *Transportgruppen*, May 1943 [3]

***Stab*/TG 1**	formed from *Stab*/KGrzbV 1
I./TG 1	formed from I./KGzbV 1
II./TG 1	formed from II./KGzbV 1
III./TG 1	formed from III./KGzbV 1
IV./TG 1	formed from IV./KGzbV 1
***Stab*/TG 2**	formed from *Stab.*/KGrzbV 3
I./TG 2	formed from KGrzbV 600
II./TG 2	formed from KGrzbV 800
III./TG 2	formed from KGrzbV 106
***Stab*/TG 3**	formed from *Stab*/KGzbV 2
I./TG 3	formed from KGrzbV 9
II./TG 3	formed from KGrzbV 50
III./TG 3	formed from KGrzbV 102
IV./TG 3	formed from I./KGzbV 172
***Stab*/TG 4**	formed from KGzbV '*Süd*'
I./TG 4	formed from KGrzbV 105
II./TG 4	formed from KGrzbV 500
III./TG 4	formed from KGrzbV 400
IV./TG 4	formed from KGrzbV 700
***Stab*/TG 5**	formed from KGrzbV '*Nord*'
I./TG 5	formed from I./KGzbV 323
II./TG 5	formed from II./KGzbV 323
III./TG 5	formed from III./KGzbV 323
TGr 10	formed from KGrzbV 5
TGr 20	formed from KGrzbV 108
TGr 30	Parts already in existence; formed from KGrzbV 23 in March 1943
Ergänzungstransportfliegergruppe	formed from KGrzbV 300

After the Axis collapse in Tunisia, the Allies were able to establish airfields along the coastline of North Africa and, in addition to the medium bombers employed hitherto, four-engined B-17 heavy bombers arrived from England. Soon, the bombers were attacking targets in Sicily and mainland Italy where airfields became priority targets and many Axis machines were destroyed on the ground. This scene of devastation was recorded on one of the airfields around Foggia in mainland Italy.

3. The units shown were the main formations created in May 1943 from the existing Kampfgruppen zur besonderen Verwendung. A few other units were added later.

Tactical Markings

As stated in the main text, until the *Transportverbände* were reorganised and a permanent force of such aircraft was created in May 1943, most transport units were formed on a temporary basis and existed only for as long as they were required at the front. Thus, before every important operation, units were called up and temporarily formed into operational *Gruppen* from formations either already in the field or from training schools and other second-line establishments by the *Kommandoweg*, or Command Method.

The basic unit was therefore the *Gruppe* and not the *Geschwader*, although on some occasions, when several *Gruppen* were operating in the same area or theatre, they were sometimes combined under a single *Geschwader Stab* but still retained their independent *Gruppe* designations and operational codes. For example, when *Kampfgeschwader* zbV 'Ahlfeld' was created in August 1939 for the invasion of Poland, it comprised aircraft from II. and III./KGzbV 1 using the operational code 1Z, parts of II./KGzbV 2 using the code G6 and further aircraft from KGzbV 172 using the code N3.

Thus, when *Gruppen* were brought together under a *Geschwader*, they were still regarded as independent units operating under an appropriate command. No new *Geschwader* code was allocated, but each component *Gruppe* was instead allocated its own unit code. However, under this arrangement, some difficulties were created when aircraft, allocated to a *Gruppe* for a particular operation, returned to their parent schools and were then called up yet again before any of the older markings could be overpainted or new ones applied. The confusing markings situation that might result is well illustrated by the experience of KGrzbV 400. When this *Gruppe* was created under *Major* Pfister on 7 December 1941, aircraft allocated to it by the *Kommandoweg* arrived from at least 25 different schools, and of these, some machines still had their four-letter radio call signs while others retained the operational codes of units to which they had previously been allocated.

To illustrate this point further, records on I./KGrzbV 172 show that while operating in North Africa in 1943, the aircraft of the *Stab* and 3. *Staffel* all carried codes beginning G6 + and with *Staffel* letters indicating that they had been drawn from I./KGzbV 2, while the majority of aircraft from 1., 2. and 4./KGrzbV 172 had four-letter radio call signs, although there was at least one aircraft with the 4V+ code of KGrzbV 9. The effect of this on ground staff who were marshalling and loading aircraft on a busy airfield and who were already under pressure to load and despatch aircraft as rapidly as possible, yet were confronted with machines from several *Gruppen*, all marked with various codes, was, understandably, one of some confusion. Fortunately, however, in the autumn of 1941, a solution to this problem was devised by the Technical Officer of KGrzbV 400, *Lt.* Gerhard Wasserkampf, who set out to introduce some uniformity to the situation.

Lt. Wasserkampf's idea was largely to disregard the unit code as its significance had, in any case, been lost. Instead, he devised a system of rudder markings combined into a tactical code. These comprised a large letter, usually the first letter in the *Kommandeur's* name, to indicate the *Gruppe* to which the machine had been assigned, a number representing the *Staffel* within the *Gruppe*, and a small letter which was the aircraft's new individual identification letter.

This basic concept of tactical rudder markings was soon adopted by other *Transporter* units experiencing marking and marshalling problems. As the use of tactical codes increased, the name of a location where the unit was first assembled or had its headquarters was sometimes substituted for the name of the commanding officer. Examples are W for Wittstock and N for Neapel, i.e. Naples. Other variations include the letter Z used by III./KGzbV 1 which had its origin in the *Geschwader* code 1Z.

Sometimes, the tactical marking system was adapted by units with difficulties less acute than those mentioned above but which still required a quick and simple means of recognition. During the Demyansk operation, for example, the aircraft of KGrzbV 9 simply carried a 9 painted on the rudder, while in another operation, aircraft of other units carried only the last two letters of their fuselage code on the fin, i.e. the individual aircraft letter and the *Staffel* letter. Examples of the letters and numbers used in tactical codes, together with their derivation, where known, are shown in the accompanying table.

This table also includes the operational unit codes employed by the various *Transporter* units, but note, however, the fundamental

RIGHT: Lt. Gerhard Wasserkampf, the Technical Officer of KGrzbV 400, who devised the system of tactical rudder codes.

ABOVE: Since transport units were frequently hastily assembled for special operations, the tactical markings were not always consistent with the aircraft's unit code. This resulted from the policy of forming transport units from training or communications establishments but incorporating elements from Gruppen with operational experience. Many aircraft still bore factory markings, as on this Ju 52/3m DE+TY over the Mediterranean, suggesting that it had probably been called up from a training unit, while the tactical code P1T on the rudder indicates it had then been assigned to 1./KGrzbV 400.

importance of the *Staffel* letter in determining a unit, for example as shown in particular by the repeated use of the fuselage codes 4V, G6 and 9P. In each instance, although the same code was used by several different *Gruppen*, the precise unit may be determined only from the *Staffel* letter. Note also that as each *Gruppe* consisted of a *Stab* and four *Staffeln*, the *Staffel* letters for air transport units differed from most other formations and required the use of *Staffel* letters not normally employed by other *Luftwaffe* formations. The letter Q, for example, had to be introduced for the 16th *Staffel* in a *Geschwader*, i.e. the fourth *Staffel* in the IV. *Gruppe*.

When Me 323s first appeared in Italy and Tunisia, they were identified by their *Stammkennzeichen*, but from the end of January 1943 they began to adopt tactical rudder codes beginning Z1 or Y1. Although yet to be confirmed, there is some evidence to suggest that, at first, the third letter was allocated from the last letter of the aircraft's *Stammkennzeichen*. Thus the tactical code X1A corresponded with the *Stammkennzeichen* DT+IA; X1B was DT+IB; X1N was DT+IN; and X1T was DT+IT. Later, however, in the *Stammkennzeichen* series beginning RD+Q, the fourth letter no longer related to the last letter of the tactical code. Thus, aircraft marked X1U, X1W and X1Z had the *Stammkennzeichen* RD+QM, RD+QB and RD+QL, respectively. It is possible that the original system became impractical when replacement aircraft arrived with *Stammkennzeichen* in which the last letter already existed. Such an example might have arisen when aircraft SG+RA was received. As the code X1A had already been allocated to DT+IA, SG+RB received the code Y1M.

Although the use of tactical codes began during the winter of 1941/1942, they proved most useful during the end of 1942 and early 1943. Eventually, because of the simplicity of the system, it was adopted by the regular transport units, as opposed to those put together on a temporary basis. Indeed, some units are known to have continued using rudder codes until well into 1944, but in these instances, the fuselage code and *Staffel* letter was generally used as a basis for the tactical code and both remained constant.

In conclusion, it may be said when examining photographs or other records from the period, that where the tactical code corresponds to the unit code, then the unit may be ascertained quite simply, but where the individual aircraft letter in the tactical code does *not* correspond with the fuselage code or four-letter *Stammkennzeichen*, then the unit may only be determined from the tactical code.

Tactical and Operational Markings

Unit Code	Staffel Letter	Tactical Code	Derivation of Tactical Letter, where known	Unit	Aircraft Operated	Remarks
B1	A			*Transport Staffel /I. Fliegerkorps*	Ju 52	Also known as *Transportstaffel* Don
N1				*Grossraumtransport Staffel*	Ju 352, Fw 200	After 30 January 1945
V1	A-B			*Transportstaffel* VIII. *Fliegerkorps*	Ju 52	
1Z	A			Stab/KGzbV 1	Ju 52 and other types	From May 1943, Stab/TG 1
1Z	B-H-K-L-M			I./KGzbV 1	Ju 52	From May 1943, I./TG 1
1Z	C-N-P-R-S			II./KGzbV 1	Ju 52	From May 1943, II./TG 1
1Z	D-T-U-V-W	Z/P	Z from unit code	III./KGzbV 1	Ju 52, SM 82	Tactical code after December 1942; from May 1943, III./TG 1
1Z	D	Z	From unit code	Savoia *Staffel*	SM 82	From May 1943, *Tr.Fl.Staffel* 4
1Z	F-X-Y-Z-Q	D		IV./KGzbV 1	Ju 52	From May 1943, IV./TG 1
1Z				TG 1	Ju 52, SM 82	After May 1943
A2	A			*Flugber./Luftgau Kdo.* Finnland	Ju 52 and other types	
C3	H			S1 *Transport Staffel/II.Fliegerkorps*	Ju 52	
N3	B-H-K-L-M			KGrvbV 172	Ju 52	N3 used until early 1941, then 4V
S3	H-K-L-M			TGr. 30	He 111	
4F	A-B-C-D-E	P	*Major* Pfister	KGrzbV 400	Ju 52	Tactical code used Dec 1941- Nov 1942; 4F from Sept 1942
4F	A-B-C-D-E	H	*Major* Hornung	KGrzbV 400	Ju 52	Tactical code from Dec 1942; after May 1943, III./TG 4
H4	A			Stab/LLG 1	Ju 52 and other types	
H4	B-H-K-L-M			I./LLG 1	Ju 52 and other types	
H4	C-N-P-R-S			II./LLG 1	Ju 52 and other types	
H4	D-T-U-V-W			III./LLG 1	Ju 52 and other types	
J4	H			LTSta. 290 and LTSta. 5	Ju 290, Ju 90, Ju 252, Pi 108	From August 1944, 14./TG 4

Code	Letters			Unit	Aircraft	Remarks
P4	H			Transport Staffel/ Fliegerführer Nord (Ost)	Ju 52	
4Q	H			Verbindungs Staffel 7. Fliegerdivision	Ju 52, and other types	Later Aufkl. St./XI. Fliegerkorps
4V	B-H-K-L-M	9		From unit designation KGrzbV 9	Ju 52	From May 1943, I./TG 3
4V	C-N-P-R-S	H	Major Heyer	KGrzbV 106	Ju 52, Go 244	
4V	D-T-U-V-W	N	Naepel (Naples)	KGrzbV 172	Ju 52	From May 1943, IV./TG 3
4V				TG 3	Ju 52 and other types	After May 1943
X4	H	S	See	LTSta. (See) 222	Bv 222	
Z4				Transport Staffel/Fliegerführer 3	Ju 52	
G5	H			Transport Staffel/V. Fliegerkorps	Ju 52	
L5	B-H-K-L-M			KGrzbV 5	He 111	From late 1942
L5	R			7./Erg. TG	Ar 232	August 1943 - August 1944, then 14./TG 4
P5		H		Sonderstaffel Transozean	Do 26, Ha 139 and other types	September 1939 - May 1940
C6	B-H-K-L-M			KGrzbV 600	Ju 52	After May 1943, I./TG 2
C6	H			Transport Staffel/Fliegerführer 4	G 12, Fi 156, Ju 52	C6 from February 1944
G6				KGzbV 2	Ju 52	August - September 1939
G6	B-H-K-L-M			KGrzbV 101	Ju 52	
G6	C-N-P-R-S	E		KGrzbV 102	Ju 52	From May 1943, III./TG 3
G6	D-T-U-V-W			KGrzbV 104	Ju 52, Go 244	From January 1943, II./KGzbV 323
G6	F-X-Y-Z-Q			KGrzbV 105	Ju 52	From May 1943, I./TG 4
G6				TG 4	Ju 52 and other types	From May 1943
J6	B-H-K-L-M	B	Major Beckmann	KGrzbV 500	Ju 52	After May 1943, II./TG 4
N6	H			Verband Major Babekuhl	Ju 52	Under Fliegerführer XI. Fliegerkorps
F7	A-B-H-K			I./LLG 2	Ju 52 and other types	
7U	B-H-K-L-M			KGrzbV 108	Ju 52 and other types	From May 1943, TGr. 20
7V	A-B-C-D-E*	7	From unit designation	KGrzbV 700	Ju 52, Leo 451	*Used as the third letter of the code. From May 1943, IV./TG 4.
8A	J	W		LTSta. (See) 1	Ju 52 See	
C8	B-E-F-G X1			I./KGzbV 323	Me 323	From late January to May 1943, then I./TG 5. Third letter of tactical code from last letter of Stammkennzeichen
C8	C-N-P-R	Y1		II./KGzbV 323	Me 323	From late January to May 1943, then II./TG 5. Third letter of tactical code from last letter of Stammkennzeichen
G8	H			Transport Staffel/IV. Fliegerkorps	Ju 52	
8T	B-H-K-L-M	T	From code '8T'	KGrzbV 800	Ju 52	From May 1943, II./TG 2
8T				TG 2	Ju 52	After May 1943
8U	C			Stab/Transport Staffel Fliegerführer 2	Ju 52 and other types	
X8	H			Flugber. RLM Staaken	Ju 52 and other types	
9G	B-K-L-M			Unknown	Ju 52	Early- Mid 1940
H9	H			LTSta. (See) 7	Latécoère 631, SNCASE 200	February - May 1944
N9	A			Flugber. Norwegen	Ju 52	9P before January 1941, then 4V
9P	B-H-K-L-M			KGrzbV 40	Ju 52	From January 1941
9P	C-N-P-R-S			KGrzbV 50	Ju 52	From January 1941
9P	D-T-U-V-W			KGrzbV 60	Ju 52	From January 1941
		K	Major Kupschuss	KGrzbV Frankfurt	Ju 52	November 1942 - March 1943. Unit withdrawn March 1943, aircraft taken over by KGzbV 106
		W	Wittstock	KGzbV Wittstock	Ju 52	November 1942 - February 1943. Unit withdrawn March 1943, aircraft taken over by KGzbV 106
C6	B-H-K-L-M	600	From unit designation	KGrzbV 600	Ju 52	December 1941 - May 1943, then I./TG 2

ABOVE: Tactical markings on a Ju 52/3m W.Nr. 5379 at Rhodes in March 1943. Reference to the table on pages 116/117 will show that the large letter T was used at that time by KGzbV 800. The 2 is the Staffel number and the small G the individual aircraft letter.

LEFT: The tactical rudder code and the Staffel letter T on the fuselage of this burned out machine in Tunisia are consistent and indicate that the machine had belonged to 1./KGzbV 172.

ABOVE: These tail units were found at El Aouina and belonged to Ju 52/3ms destroyed during the airlift to Tunisia. Those with a large letter W belonged to aircraft operating under KGrzbV 'Wittstock' and that with the K came from a machine allocated to KGrzbV 'Frankfurt'. Also seen is a single example with the T of KGrzbV 800.

The Final Rounds in the Mediterranean

Following the Axis surrender in Tunisia on 13 May 1943, German air transport units in the Mediterranean succeeded in evacuating most of the German personnel from the Italian island fortress of Pantelleria, situated between Tunis and Sicily, before it was invaded and surrendered on 11 June. With the Allies now controlling virtually the whole coastline of North Africa, it was obvious to the German High Command that the prospect of the enemy opening a second front somewhere on Italian territory was a distinct possibility. However, while uncertain when and where this would take place, the German leaders concluded that Sicily, Sardinia and Corsica were the most likely alternatives and that the garrisons there were, therefore, to be strengthened.

The effort to reinforce Sicily was carried out on a relatively minor scale as the situation in Russia had left only some 80 Ju 52/3ms and 20 Me 323s remaining in Italy, these being distributed among IV./TG 1 and III./TG 2 with *Stab*/TG 4, and IV./TG 3 with *Stab*, I. and II./TG 5, although the latter *Gruppe* was not yet fully equipped. Further units were held in France, but many of these were engaged in very comprehensive training which included large-scale parachute and airborne exercises, some involving glider landings with parachute braking and retro-rockets. The units in France were I. and II./TG 1, III./TG 4, IV./TG 4, newly converted to LeO 451 aircraft, TGr 30, KGrzbV 25 flying He 111s temporarily withdrawn from training and the whole of LLG 1 and LLG 2 with a fleet of DFS 230, Me 321, and Go 242 gliders. The airborne forces in France included 1. *Fallschirmjäger Division* and, still being formed, 2. *Fallschirmjäger Division*.

When the threatened attack finally materialised with the first Allied landings on Sicily on 10 July 1943, 1. *Fallschirmjäger Division* was immediately ordered to reinforce regular and airborne forces already on the island by every possible method. In order that paratroops could be transported with all their equipment, weapons and ammunition, this included the large-scale use of gliders. The 1. *Fallschirmjäger Division* was dropped or landed in this way in a series of operations beginning on the 14th, on which date the troops of FJR 3 jumped south of Catania from the He 111s of TGr 30 and Ju 52/3ms of TG 1. This was followed three days later by FJR 4 and, subsequently, by similar small-scale parachute operations to the north of Catania and along the north coast which, owing to a fuel shortage, took place over a period of about a month.

Re-supply operations were attempted by some 100 Ju 52/3ms operating from mainland Italy which landed or dropped containers. Go 242s were also employed, mainly to transport heavy weapons, and on 20 and 27 July, 14 of these gliders from LLG 2 landed on the beaches near Faro. Re-supply was greatly hampered by the vigilance of Allied fighters which shot down 15 Ju 52/3ms on 18 July and another ten carrying weapons and troops on the 25th. More satisfactory as supply aircraft were the

ABOVE: In the fighting which followed the Allied landings in Sicily on 10 July 1943, the German units fought well and mounted vigorous counter-attacks on 11 and 12 July. Among the prisoners taken in the often prolonged and bitter defence of certain key positions were these Fallschirmjäger who had fought near the Primo Sole bridge, a 122 metre long structure which changed hands several times.

LEFT: Following the Allied invasion of Sicily, 14 Go 242 gliders from LLG 2 were used on 20 and 27 July to land heavy weapons on the beach near Faro.

He 111s of TGr 30 which dropped supplies as well as being employed as glider tugs. A total of some 3,000 men was brought to Sicily by air transport, while special weapons, such as anti-tank guns, were dropped in containers or flown in by glider.

Although the Italians evacuated Sicily in some disorder between 3 and 16 August, the Germans fought an excellent rearguard action which allowed them to evacuate the bulk of their troops across the Straits of Messina to Italy before the end of the campaign on 17 August.

The invasion of mainland Italy began with British diversionary attacks in the toe of Italy on 3 September, followed by a major Anglo-American landing at Salerno on the 9th. The German High Command was by now very well aware that the Italians' morale was faltering and believed that they might at any moment lay down their arms and defect to the Allies. As a precaution, the 2. *Fallschirmjäger Division* had already been brought to the Rome area, so that when the Italian dictator Benito Mussolini was arrested and the Italian Government announced a capitulation on 10 September, this *Division* immediately went into action and occupied Rome. Major resistance was encountered only near Monte Rotondo, where II./FJR 6 jumped to seize the Italian Headquarters.

At the same time, Hitler ordered *Generaloberst* Kurt Student to rescue Mussolini before he could be handed over to the Allies. Although the force assembled included S*turmbannführer* Otto Skorzeny and 16 men of the *Waffen-SS*, the rescue plan was devised by Student who had learned that the Italians had taken Mussolini to a mountain hotel on the Gran Sasso mountain. The rescue operation took place on 12 September, when some ten DFS 230s of LLG 1 carrying the troops of the *Fallschirmjäger Lehr Bataillon*, landed on a plateau on the Gran Grasso, while the main force, I./FJR 7, came up by road and secured the foot of the plateau. The operation was a complete success and the rescued Mussolini, who had been handed over by his Italian guards without any opposition, was flown to safety in an Fi 156 and then taken by He 111 to Munich where he was greeted by the *Führer*.

In Sardinia, the German withdrawal was completed by 19 September and, although air transport was employed to a small extent, was largely effected by sea and in good order. The evacuation of Corsica was hampered by a shortage of aircraft owing to other commitments and poor serviceability, which resulted in only some 80 Ju 52/3ms, a few SM.82s and one Me 323 *Gruppe* being available. Units taking part in the evacuation of the islands were II./TG 5 with Me 323s, the Savoia *Staffel* at Grosseto with SM.82s, and the Ju 52/3m *Gruppen* II. and III./TG 1, based respectively at Florence and Pistoia; II./TG 2 at Pontedera; III./TG 2 at Lucca, and III./TG 4 at Pisa but with few aircraft. The III./TG 2 also had few aircraft and had begun converting to SM.82s seized by the Germans when the Italians defected. The benefits of the large number of Italian aircraft which fell into German hands at this time and which were later put into service were, however, of short duration as supplies of spare parts and equipment proved inadequate. But at least the Germans no longer had to contend with the Italians and the lack of harmony that had earlier rendered cooperation with them very difficult. Freed from such constraints, the Germans were now able to operate in the theatre more decisively and with complete independence.

During the operation to evacuate Corsica, some 27,000 men are believed to have been removed by air, including an Italian parachute regiment which elected to remain with the German troops in spite of Italy's defection. The bulk of the heavy equipment, motor transport, armour, etc, was successfully transported by sea, but rapid air evacuation of a number of personnel and equipment still on Corsica was required when French troops landed there on 14 September. During the course of the operation, which was completed on 5 October, the Allies claimed to have shot down 26 Ju 52/3ms and four SM.82s. Although these figures are believed to be too high, it is known that a very successful Allied bombing programme, combined with the use of inexperienced German crews, accounted for at least as many aircraft on the ground and in crashes as were lost to Allied fighters.

During the evacuation of Corsica, aircraft were parked at night and widely dispersed on airfields as far inland as possible in Italy to minimise the danger from Allied bombing attacks. In order to increase the effort, bomber units were ordered to assist in supplying crews for SM.82s newly captured in North Italy, but their inexperience in handling this aircraft resulted in a very large number of crashes. The SM.82 also had a reputation for easily burning, so when an engine caught fire on this example, believed to have belonged to the Savoia Staffel attached to TG 1, the flames quickly spread to the fuselage and the machine was completely destroyed.

ABOVE: TG 5 was an exception to the general rule that all Transport Geschwader comprised a Stab and four Gruppen each with 12 aircraft. Instead, TG 5 comprised only three Gruppen, each with a Stabsstaffel and three Staffeln each with six Me 323s. Here, a Marder self-propelled gun is being reversed into the cargo hold of an Me 323 D-6 of I./TG 5 during the reinforcement of Sicily, this particular aircraft being W.Nr. 1142 which was allocated the operational code C8+AB. The Marder weighed just less than 12 tons and was an anti-tank gun mounted on the chassis of a PzKpfw II.

BELOW: Due to the height of its six 1100 hp Gnome-Rhône 14 M engines, servicing the Me 323 required the use of a special trestle.

ABOVE: The burned-out remains of an Me 323 D-1 of 3./TG 5 in Italy. This aircraft carried the operational markings C8+AP on the fuselage and first arrived in Italy in July 1943. It was damaged during a bombing raid soon afterwards near Mantua, but after being repaired it later made a forced landing at Pomigliano following engine failure in bad weather. The aircraft remained at Pomigliano when the Germans withdrew and was photographed by advancing US forces. Although the fuselage Balkenkreuz has been removed as a souvenir, the individual aircraft letter A may still be seen. Note the tactical code Y1H on the rudder.

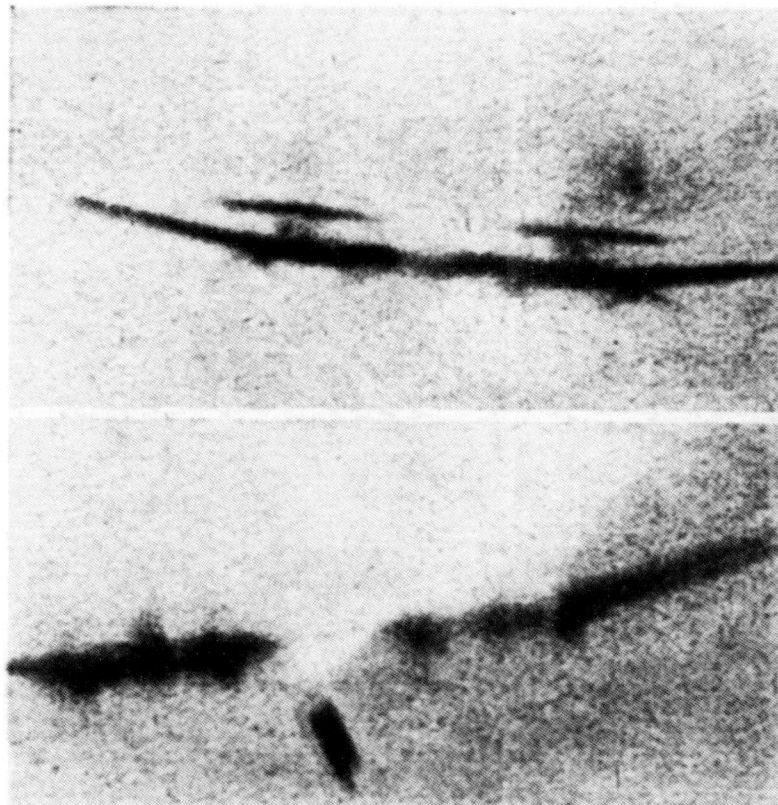

RIGHT: Some German troop units stationed in the south of France were air-lifted to Italy in a variety of aircraft including gliders towed by He 111 Zs. These gun camera stills show an He 111 Z which was attacked and shot down by a Mosquito.

RIGHT: On 23 July 1943, Ofw. Hans-Georg Boldt of Lufttransport-staffel 290 took off from Pisa in this Ju 90 coded J4+JH, W.Nr. 0007, for a flight to Borgo in Corsica. As he neared the island, however, he was intercepted by an RAF B-26, from which this photograph was taken. The Ju 90 escaped serious damage and continued on its flight to Corsica where it was then mistaken for an Allied aircraft. When the right outer engine was hit by the island's light Flak, the machine lost height and crash-landed in shallow water close to the beach at Bastia.

LEFT: This Me 323 should have taken off from France as part of a formation of similar aircraft ordered to Rome on 30 July 1943 but it was delayed by engine trouble and set out alone. It was subsequently attacked at low level over the sea near Corsica and the pilot, Ofw. Walter Honig of II./TG 5, was obliged to make an emergency landing on Corsica. This photograph was taken from the attacking aircraft, an RAF B-26 of 14 Sqn.

1943-1945

ABOVE AND LEFT: This severely damaged and cannibalised Me 323 D-2 is believed to have been W.Nr. 1235 of I./TG 5 which carried the operational code C8+GP and was found on Menfi airfield, near Castelvetrano in Sicily, in 1943. Note that most national insignia have been removed as souvenirs and that the swastikas have been overpainted. The I. and II./TG 5 officially left the Mediterranean theatre on 1 October 1943 and III./TG 5 served only in the East.

RIGHT: When the Allied advance in Italy compelled German units to retreat northwards, unserviceable aircraft which could not be flown away were destroyed with demolition charges to prevent them from falling into enemy hands. Photographed in Italy in October, and clearly showing signs of being deliberately destroyed, was this Ju 52/3m with the engines and entire forward section burned out. Although the full unit code cannot be seen, this aircraft was certainly 4V+ER of 7./TG 3. Note the tactical code T7E on the rudder in yellow.

BELOW: Following the Italian armistice in September 1943, the Luftwaffe seized large numbers of machines which had formerly seen service with the Regia Aeronautica. This SM.82 has been repainted in Luftwaffe camouflage and markings.

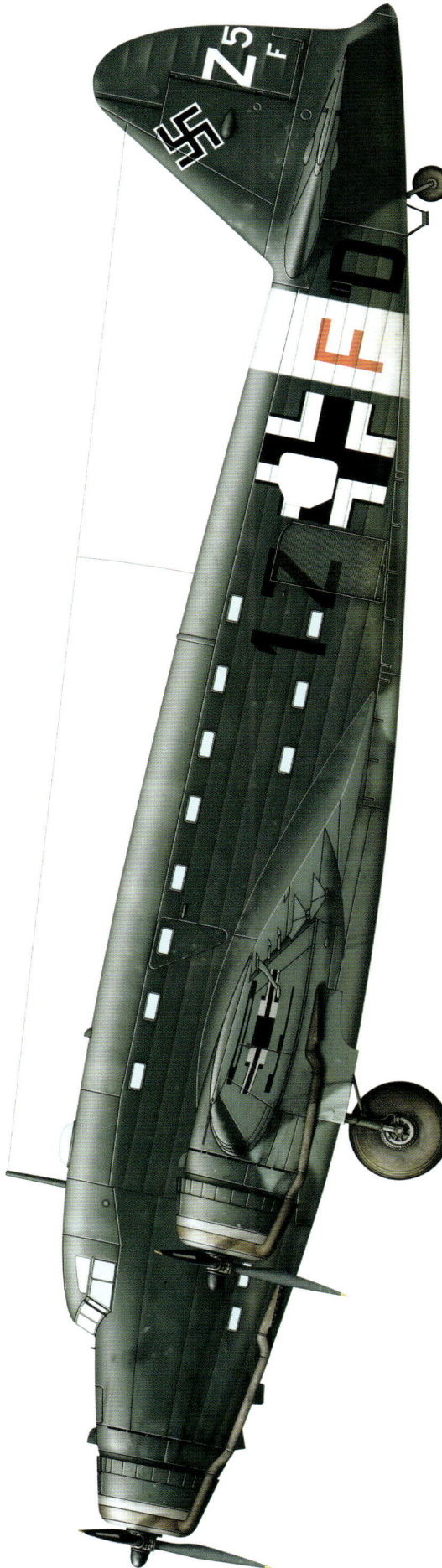

Savoia-Marchetti SM.82 IZ+FD of the Savoia Staffel of TG 1, Italy, Summer 1943

The uppersurfaces on this aircraft were finished overall in RLM 71, but with slight colour variations due to weathering. Undersurfaces were in RLM 65 and the tactical code Z5F was painted on the rudder. The individual aircraft letter F on the fuselage was in red and the tips of propeller blades were yellow.

THIS PAGE: Apart from the names of girlfriends or wives, personal markings featuring females are almost unknown on Luftwaffe aircraft, making the decoration applied to the SM.73 flown by Fw. Edmund Lück of 10./TG 1, (*RIGHT*) extremely rare. In the photograph (*BELOW*) the artwork may be seen being applied to the white fuselage band of Fw. Lück's IZ+CU, while the views (*BOTTOM LEFT AND BOTTOM RIGHT*) show the finished result. Lück was killed when his aircraft was shot down between Pisa and Corsica on 26 September 1943.

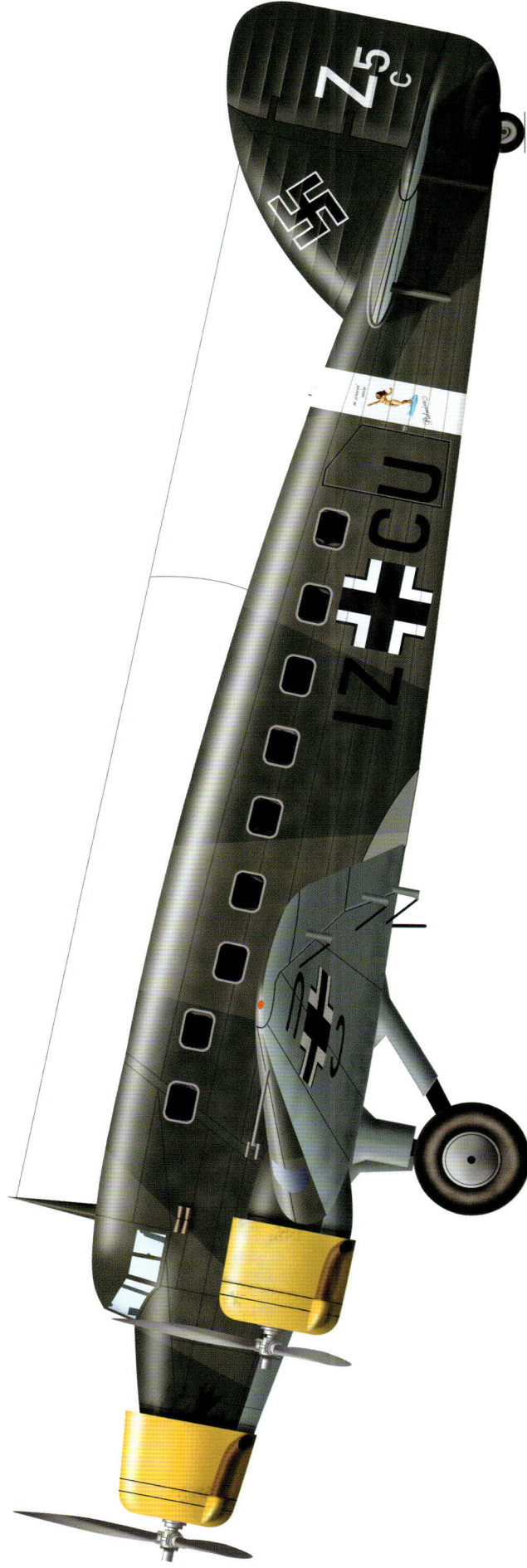

u sciuri miu

Palmira

**Personal emblem of
Fw. Edmund Lück.**

SM.73 flown by Fw. Edmund Lück of 10./TG 1, Italy, Summer 1943

The uppersurfaces on this aircraft were finished in a splinter scheme of two greens which, if not 70 and 71, are believed to have been close equivalents in Italian paints. The undersurfaces were 65 or similar with all national insignia to standard Luftwaffe dimensions and proportions. Note the yellow engine cowlings and the tactical code Z5C in white on the rudder. The inscription 'u sciuri miu Palmira' translates as, 'To my flower, Palmira'.

Transport Operations on the Southern Sector of the Eastern Front

When the German attempt to seize the initiative at Kursk in July 1943 failed in the face of a Soviet counter-attack, it marked the beginning of much larger Soviet offensives from the Baltic to the Black Sea, and during the remainder of 1943 the Germans suffered enormous territorial losses. In the south, Kharkov was lost on 23 August, and by 22 September Soviet units had begun to cross the Dniepr south of Kiev. By the end of September, the Soviets had reached the Kerch Strait, forcing the German Seventeenth Army, which had been holding a large bridgehead in the Kuban, to withdraw its forces across the Kerch Strait and into the Crimea. This was achieved with complete success, but on 24 October, the Soviet advance to the Dniepr had allowed them to occupy the Perekop Isthmus, the strip of land separating the Crimea from the mainland.

The Army and the Luftwaffe considered the Go 242 a most satisfactory freight glider on account of its easy access for loading and its large hold which was capable of accommodating 3,500 kg of cargo. This example was photographed near Kharkov in the early summer of 1943 and shows how the rear fuselage could be raised to allow access to the interior. Note the position of the Stammkennzeichen and the Balkenkreuz and the yellow band on the rear fuselage.

Although Seventeenth Army was now isolated, Hitler ordered that for political, economic and military reasons, the Crimea was to be held at all costs. The Army was therefore to be strengthened with men and equipment flown in by a transport force assembled for the purpose on three main airfields at Odessa I, II and III. Although Odessa II had a concrete runway, it was too thin to permit fully-loaded Me 323s to land and take off and had to be reinforced before it could be used. At Odessa III, the constant stream of aircraft during the muddy and thaw periods soon furrowed the taxiing area to a depth of about 16 inches, but as operations had to continue, the transport crews had no choice but to use the airfield. Soon it was purely a matter of luck whether the fully-laden Ju 52/3ms could lift off before they reached the end of the runway. Conditions were made more difficult by the sudden and unpredictable changes in the weather, usually accompanied by heavy fogs, which restricted flying.

Two *Gruppen*, I. and III./TG 2, arrived from the Mediterranean theatre to take part in the operation in October, but as they had not been informed beforehand of the area in which they were to operate, they had left behind all the emergency equipment necessary for flights over water. Nor had these *Gruppen* been adequately equipped for winter operations and they lacked the necessary de-icing equipment and felt-lined covers to protect engines from the severe cold. Although the services of these units was urgently required, a week elapsed before de-icing equipment could be installed and the crews provided with inflatable rafts and life jackets.

Flights to the Crimea were at first fairly routine, the usual loads being troops returning from leave, aircraft fuel, bombs and equipment, while wounded and any authorised non-essential personnel were flown out on the return flights. The level of activity remained within reasonable limits, and with the Soviets preoccupied with developments in the southern mainland, opposition was light and enabled operations to be carried out in daylight.

Meanwhile, Soviet advances on the southern sectors of the main front had resulted in a very dangerous situation. German Army units were under severe pressure but short of ammunition, land supply routes were poor, and an unusually mild winter had resulted in very muddy conditions which impeded operations. The air supply of the Crimea had therefore barely begun when the *Transportflieger* were drawn into several other, almost simultaneous, operations in the Ukraine.

The first of these was in October when supplies were flown to elements of the Eighth and Sixth Armies, then engaged in heavy defensive fighting on a sector of the front running from east of Kirovograd to Nikopol. Operating in this area were I. and III./TG 2, II. and III./TG 3, and I./TG 4, all equipped with Ju 52s, plus I./TG 5 with Me 323s. Also available was III./TG 1 with SM.82s, but this aircraft was found to be unsuitable for operations in winter and, combined with a difficulty in obtaining spares, resulted in the type being temporarily withdrawn.

On 24 December 1943, a Soviet offensive opened against the German Army Group South and for some time the *Wehrmacht* communiqués made daily mention of the heavy fighting, serious threats and

German withdrawal in Southern Russia, December 1943 to Mid-April 1944

Map legend:
- German Pockets
- Front Line 23 December 1943
- Front Line Mid April 1944
- Country borders

Map labels: Bobruisk, Brest-Litovsk, Gomel, POLAND, Jasionka, Krosno, Lvov, Zhitomir, Kiev, Kharkov, SLOVAKIA, Tarnopol, Kanev, Proskurov, Buchach, Chertkov, Korsun, GRUPPE STEMMERMANN, Cherkassy, Carpathian Mountains, Kamenets-Podolski, FIRST PZ ARMY, Vinnitsa, HUNGARY, Uman, Dniepr River, Prut River, Yampol, UKRAINE, Kirovograd, Stalino, Bug River, Golta, Zaporozhye, Nikopol, Dniestr River, Odessa, Kherson, Perekop, Sea of Azov, RUMANIA, Zilistea, Galati, Buzau, Kerch, CRIMEA, Black Sea, Constanta, Sevastopol, Chersones, BULGARIA

costly critical situations on the Kirovograd sector of operations. Everywhere the Germans were forced back from the river Dniepr except for an area between Kanev and Cherkassy, south of Kiev, which formed a dangerous German salient projecting eastwards. On 28 January 1944, elements of the German Eighth Army comprising some 56,000 troops in this salient – the equivalent of six and a half divisions and which included the *SS Division 'Wiking'* and the independent Belgian *SS Brigade 'Wallonie'* – were encircled within an area near Cherkassy, south of Kiev. This was referred to in the *OKW* communiqués as the 'Cherkassy pocket' but is more accurately known as the 'Korsun pocket'. These formations, later placed under the overall command of *General* Wilhelm Stemmermann, were compressed into an area that at no point was more than 35 kilometres wide.

In the light of the Stalingrad experience, plans were immediately set in motion for a relief force to break through to the trapped *Gruppe* Stemmermann, which itself lost no time in preparing to break out. The existing air supply operations to the front were stepped up, and responsibility for supplying the pocket was entrusted to a special staff working with VIII. *Fliegerkorps* in the Zhitomir area. Supply

operations to the encircled troops began on 31 January, the units taking part being I., II. and III./TG 3 under *Major* Hans-Hermann Ellerbrock, *Major* Otto Baumann and *Major* Paul Risch respectively. Take-off airfields at the beginning of the operation were at Uman, Golta and Proskurov.

As Soviet aircraft were particularly active over the encircled area, one of the *Transportgruppen's* first tasks was to bring in a light anti-aircraft battery for the defence of the landing ground at Korsun. The Soviets had likewise established their own anti-aircraft defences immediately following the encirclement, and although the transport aircraft frequently altered their approach and return routes, they were constantly exposed to ground fire from all types of light weapons. At first, operations were carried out at low altitude and in close formation, the machines sometimes descending to hedge-hopping height, but on one occasion, *Major* Paul Risch, who had earlier been placed in charge of all units engaged in the operation, encountered such heavy anti-aircraft fire on his outward flight to the pocket that, contrary to explicit instructions to fly at low altitude, he decided to make the return flight at a greater height. As the aircraft assembled over Korsun, they were immediately attacked by a group of Soviet fighters and 12 Ju 52/3ms were shot down.

Thereafter, the role of operation leader was assigned to *Major* Baumann and flights were carried out at slightly higher altitude with fighter escort. The hard-pressed fighter force, however, could only provide a few aircraft so that formations of up to 36 Ju 52/3ms frequently set out with only three escort fighters. Fortunately, these proved sufficient to deter the Soviet fighters from attacking the transport formations and the VVS reverted instead to increasingly more frequent attacks carried out by low-flying Il-2s against the landing ground at Korsun itself. Eventually, as the landing field began to thaw during the hours of daylight, touching down became so difficult that supplies were air-dropped, although on nights when light frost again hardened the ground, each aircraft made an average of three night landings.

The weather also influenced the progress of III. *Panzer Korps,* the relief force which was slowly advancing towards *Gruppe* Stemmermann from the west. The thaw had made the roads almost impassable so that the transportation of overland supplies was virtually impossible. With their tanks consuming three times their normal amount of fuel because of the difficult conditions, crews resorted to carrying fuel up to the front in buckets and found it easier to do this barefoot than to stop every few minutes to retrieve their boots which had become stuck in the mud. The obvious solution was to supply III. *Panzer Korps*, too, by air, and sorties were flown in which ammunition, petrol and food were dropped in containers along its route of advance. As the *Panzer Korps* slowly progressed in a narrow wedge towards *Gruppe* Stemmermann, its spearhead was subjected to heavy attack on both sides by strong Soviet forces which were also favourably positioned to fire on the approaching transports. Undeterred, the pilots took every advantage of the surrounding terrain, sometimes descending to very low level in order to fly behind woods or low hills.

Mostly, the aircraft dropped their cargoes close alongside III. *Panzer Korps'* tanks and other vehicles, but if frost permitted, the

ABOVE LEFT AND ABOVE: During the unseasonably mild winter on the southern sector of the Eastern Front, snow and frost alternated with muddy conditions. These photographs are believed to have been taken in the German salient near Cherkassy, south of Kiev. When the salient was cut off in January 1944, supplying the troops in the pocket was undertaken by I., II. and III./TG 3 operating under VIII. Fliegerkorps.

BELOW: A supply drop in progress. The release of containers in this way made accurate dropping impossible, and in conditions of deep snow, exhausted troops were unable to collect the containers which could be scattered up to 550 metres from the dropping point.

LEFT: In order to avoid Soviet anti-aircraft fire when operating close to the front lines, Luftwaffe transport pilots would often descend almost to ground level in order to take advantage of any available cover, as shown by this low-flying Ju 52/3m operating near a wooded area in Russia.

BELOW: A snow camouflaged Ju 52/3m dropping supplies from low level. Generally, experience showed that when small arms ammunition was dropped without a parachute it was badly damaged and only half the amount was fit for use. Sacks containing hard fodder for horses split on impact unless reinforced with wire netting, while bread arrived broken but fit for consumption. However, during the two-week operation mounted in February 1944 in support of troops trapped in the Korsun pocket fighting their way to safety, the mud and snow of the unusually mild winter had a cushioning effect. The result was that a higher proportion of supplies dropped in this manner arrived intact.

most experienced pilots risked night landings in the open terrain along the road. Air drops with parachute containers were quickly discontinued as ground fire during the ten minutes it took to release them was too heavy and, in any event, high winds often blew them into Soviet hands. Instead, the aircraft flew at reduced speed a few metres above the ground while the cargo was pushed out of the loading door. It was found that the mud and snow so reduced the impact that when packed in heavy crates, even 75 mm and 88 mm shells could be delivered without damage. Petrol, however, could only be dropped in very robust drums, but still an average of one in every five burst on impact. During night drops, the supply aircraft were guided to the relief column by torches and vehicle headlights, which were flashed as soon as an aircraft was heard approaching.

The highest number of operations was recorded on the night of 15/16 February when, in response to a request for an increased ammunition drop, some crews flew as many as five sorties. By this time, the German pocket had been reduced to an area some 10 by 11 kilometres, but the majority of the troops were still alive. However, many were killed mercilessly in a savage, last-minute Soviet assault the following day, just as the force in the pocket made contact with the relief column. Although from this time on air supply was no longer necessary, the aircraft continued to make flights to the area, landing at two airfields along the retreat route to fly out more of the sick and wounded, or troops so exhausted they were simply incapable of dragging themselves any further.

During the course of the 17-day operation, the transports had flown a total of 1,500 sorties for the loss of 32 Ju 52/3ms and 113 damaged. More than 2,000 tons of supplies were delivered and over 2,000 sick and wounded flown out of the pocket, but the whole operation was a tragedy. Although the breakout had succeeded, the toll in terms of hardship, suffering and death was enormous. Of the original 56,000 troops in the pocket, 18,800 men were lost, and all armour, artillery and heavy equipment had been abandoned. Included among the casualties was *General* Stemmermann himself, who died of wounds sustained when the horse-drawn wagon on which he was travelling was destroyed by an anti-tank shell.

BELOW: The remains of horse-drawn transport, abandoned by troops surrounded in the Korsun pocket during their migration westwards in February 1944.

Supplying First Panzer Army

Despite their bitter resistance along the Dniepr river, German forces in the Ukraine continued to be pushed further back towards the River Bug. Most transport sorties in the area were flown to bring ammunition from Odessa to the Nikolayev area where the military situation had reached a critical stage following heavy Soviet attacks along this entire sector. Soon, further to the north-west, the Soviets had surrounded Tarnopol, while on 24 March, south-east of the city, Soviet forces wheeled to envelop the German First *Panzer* Army. Twenty-two divisions were completely surrounded in a huge pocket between the Bug and the Dniestr, and separated from the bulk of Fourth Panzer Army by a gap of over 80 kilometres. The commander of First *Panzer* Army, *General* Hans Hube, was determined to fight his way out, but Hitler at first refused permission. Only after heated arguments was permission granted to extricate the Army, but Hube's existing supplies were far from sufficient to keep the men mobile and in fighting condition. Once again, the *Transportflieger* were required to supply the surrounded force until it could reach its own lines.

The operation was assigned to *Luftflotte* 4's *Transportfliegerführer* 2, *Generalmajor* Morzik, and all transport units necessary to supply First *Panzer* Army were made available. These consisted of I./TG 1 under *Major* Oskar Schmidt; IV./TG 1 under *Major* Penkert; I./TG 3 under *Major* Hans-Hermann Ellerbrock and I./TG4 under *Obstlt.* Josef Kögel, all with Ju 52/3ms, plus the He 111s of *Major* Walter Hornung's TGr 30 and the additional He 111s and DFS 230 gliders of *Schleppgruppe* 2. These units took up positions on the take-off bases at Lvov, Krosno and Jasionka, all in southern Poland. In addition, the He 111s of I./KG 4 under *Hptm.* Ernst Göpel plus parts of KG 54 and KG 55 were placed under the command of *Transportfliegerführer* 2 for the duration of the operation. This resulted in the total availability of some 100 He 111s and 150 Ju 52/3ms.

By 25 March, most units had already arrived at their muddy and overcrowded take-off bases where they had to be refuelled by hand pumps directly from petrol drums. Despite bad weather, operations commenced the next day with the He 111s air-dropping containers and the Ju 52/3ms landing with their supplies at Proskurov, the only suitable airfield within the enclosed area. This, however, was soon left behind as the pocket migrated westwards, and the problem of finding suitable landing or air-drop areas along the route of First *Panzer* Army's retreat was overcome by parties of four trained men equipped with radio beacons, flare-path lights, marker beacons and signals flares of all kinds. These parties reconnoitred the ground along the route in Army half-tracked vehicles and selected appropriate areas. Aircraft were then guided to the troops' new position by marker beacons which, to foil Soviet decoys, were laid out in a pre-arranged pattern of crosses, circles and triangles.

It was in this way that an improvised landing ground for the Ju 52/3ms was found at Kamenets-Podolski. This was kept in use until the last possible moment, although on one occasion Russian tanks advanced to the very edge of the field, shelling the taxiing area and disrupting operations until German troops forced them to withdraw. Even then, the transport aircraft were compelled to take off low over the surrounding enemy forces.

After Kamenets-Podolski was abandoned on 2 April, the majority of supplies were air-dropped. By this time, the *Transporters* were flying only at night when weather conditions were more favourable than the snowstorms and low cloud invariably encountered during the day. The aircraft took off immediately after nightfall at intervals of between three to five minutes, depending on the skill of the various units. Morale was excellent and each crew was eager to fly as many operations as possible, often making up to four or five sorties per night.

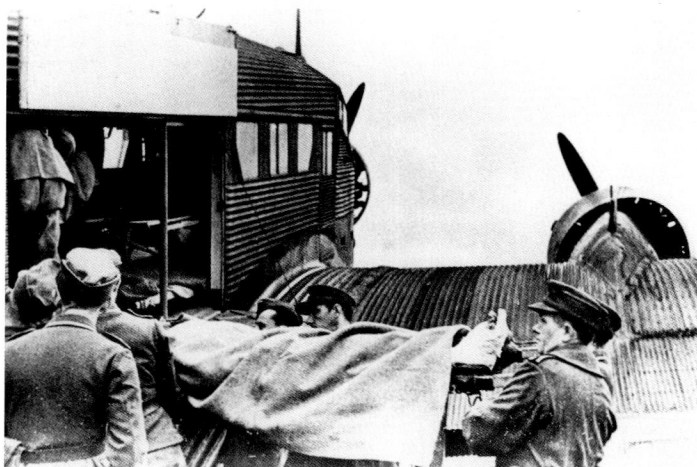

BELOW: Since it was never certain whether aircraft would be able to land during the supply of First Panzer Army, no arrangements were made to transport wounded to landing areas. However, when conditions did permit aircraft to land, any wounded who happened to be nearby could be flown out.

BELOW: A Ju 52/3m air dropping supplies. Except that such missions were normally carried out at night, First Panzer Army was supplied in this way in March and April 1944 after the improvised landing ground at Kamenets-Podolski was abandoned.

Losses due to enemy action were exceedingly light; no Soviet night fighters were encountered and even the enemy's anti-aircraft fire had little effect. Nevertheless, flight routes were changed constantly, sometimes from operation to operation, and each night an experienced crew flew an advanced sortie, reporting the areas relatively free of anti-aircraft concentrations so that the approach route could be established accordingly.

The greatest number of sorties was flown by the He 111 units, TGr 30 alone flying 1,285 sorties to drop a total of 11,020 containers with 1,670 tons of supplies. The He 111's comparatively long-range enabled it to make three flights to the encircled area before refuelling and the He 111 H-20 could carry a very worthwhile load of nine 250 kg containers, or eight 250 kg containers and one 500 kg container, on its internal racks. Sometimes, the slipstream caused these parachutes to open prematurely so that they became entangled around the tailwheel, but on one occasion, a potentially more dangerous situation arose involving an He 111 which had just taken off. Before the pilot had retracted the main undercarriage, the parachute on a container, mounted externally between the engines, opened and wrapped itself around an oleo and wheel. Fortunately, the pilot was able to release the container and made a safe emergency landing near his airfield, still with the parachute wrapped around one mainwheel.

The 250 kg containers were also carried by Ju 52/3ms, but these were stored internally and dropped manually through the loading hatch or open door. In order to free cargo space for battle supplies, the delivery of food was forbidden and the retreating First *Panzer* Army was ordered to live off the land or to requisition foodstuffs from the local population. Supplies therefore mainly consisted of ammunition, petrol and essential tank components, but as it was generally not possible to land and pick up wounded, a number of medical supply containers were also dropped.

On 8 April, after fighting its way westwards through 300 kilometres of Soviet-held territory, First *Panzer* Army linked up with II *SS Panzer Korps* (9. and 10. *SS Panzer* Divisions), which had advanced to meet it, and the last supply sorties were flown on the 10th. Although First *Panzer* Army had killed and eaten nearly all of its horses and had had to abandon most of its equipment and heavy weapons, more than 200,000 troops reached safety.

The success of the operation to the First *Panzer* Army was due to the determination of the surrounded troops, who had made a series of forced marches to escape the Soviet trap, plus the high morale of the *Transportflieger* and the long experience of the unit commanders. The *Transportflieger's* familiarity with conditions on the Eastern Front had allowed them to brave the weather and maintain a supply of fuel and ammunition sufficient to ensure that only rarely did First *Panzer* Army experience any shortages. The whole operation was therefore regarded as a success, and the air supply aspect of the operation was an impressive achievement. Regardless of the weather, the *Transporters* had flown some 8,000 sorties, during which they had delivered a total of between 3,500 and 4,000 tons of supplies, the equivalent of 200-250 tons daily.

At the same time as air transport units were assisting First *Panzer* Army in its fight out of encirclement, it became necessary to evacuate *Luftwaffe* units and equipment from airfields in the Ukraine before they were overrun by Soviet forces. In February, Uman was evacuated by the aircraft of II./TG 3 and TG 5, followed by the evacuation of the whole Ukraine. This began in earnest in the second week of March when the airfields at Proskurov, Nikolayev and Golta closed down.

When Tarnopol was finally cut off on the afternoon of 23 March, the weak garrison prepared to defend the city. The defenders, however, were particularly short of ammunition, and when an attempt to break through on the 25th failed, a comparatively small-scale supply operation was mounted by *Luftwaffe* bomber units under *Transportfliegerführer* 2 and the He 111s and DFS 230 gliders of *Hptm.* Josef Faé's *Schleppgruppe* 2.

The whole operation was made particularly difficult by the strong Soviet anti-aircraft defences and the ever decreasing size of the area held by the defenders. The main airport had already been lost, but during the first phase, the DFS 230s were able to land on a small landing strip, although heavy

An He 111, probably of TGr 30, with a supply container already mounted beneath the centre section and another in the foreground. Note the winter camouflage, which has been achieved by spraying white or RLM 76 over the original 70/71 finish in such a manner that patches of the original greens appear as mottles. In the spring of 1944, TGr 30 flew 1,285 missions during the operation to supply First Panzer Army encircled near Kamenets-Podolski.

ABOVE: Personnel and Go 242s of Schleppgruppe 2 on the Eastern Front in early 1944. Elements from this Gruppe took part in two operations to supply First Panzer Army in March 1944 and were later employed in air supply operations to German troops besieged at Tarnopol. The undersurfaces on these gliders were 65 and the uppersurfaces are thought to have been green 71 with an overspray of 02. The badge on the nose shows a bird over crossed swords against a cloud background.

anti-aircraft fire restricted operations to the early morning and evening. The gliders were towed into the air by He 111s carrying bombs as well as supply containers, so that after releasing the gliders, the Heinkels were able to attack nearby anti-aircraft batteries until the gliders had reached their target. The He 111s then released their own supply containers low over the drop area and returned to their base. For the glider pilots, however, who made extremely difficult pinpoint landings under enemy fire, there was no escape and they joined in the ground fighting.

Because of the Soviet defences, the bomber units operated at night, but the darkness, the anti-aircraft fire and the size of the drop area left no margin for error. Again, the bombers carried a mixed load of bombs to suppress Soviet anti-aircraft fire while other machines released their supplies, but the ever-decreasing size of the defended area made accurate drops very difficult. At first, the daily delivery of munitions averaged 12 to 15 tons, but when the landing area eventually fell into Soviet hands and the gliders were unable to land, daily deliveries sank to a mere eight tons. However, only a small proportion of the supply containers landed on target, and on 1 April, the commander of the city, *Generalmajor* von Neindorff, reported that of the 90 containers dropped the previous night, only five had arrived. The others, with their desperately needed ammunition and first aid supplies, had landed in enemy territory, in the city's lakes and swamps, or had been lost amid the ruins.

A second relief attack failed and the last air-drop was made on the night of 13/14 April. A breakout was attempted but was mounted too late and the majority of the troops were still trapped when resistance in Tarnopol ended on 15 April. A final radio message from the pocket was received at noon on the 15th and reported the death of von Neindorff, who had fallen in close combat.

LEFT: Lt. Hans-Joachim Valet, seen here on the right, was awarded the German Cross in Gold on 31 August 1943 and later, on 20 April 1944, he became one of the relatively few Transportflieger to receive the Ritterkreuz. On both occasions he was flying with I./TG 2, and is shown here with his Bordfunker, Fw. Herbert Blüchel.

RIGHT: A Bordschütze – an air-gunner – aboard a Ju 52/3m. Although armed only with a single ring-mounted 13 mm MG 131 or, as shown here, just a 7.9 mm MG 15, a number of Ju 52/3m air-gunners succeeded in shooting down enemy fighters. This photograph was taken in November 1943, at which time the gunners of aircraft operating in the Crimea had the additional duty of ensuring that aircraft were properly loaded.

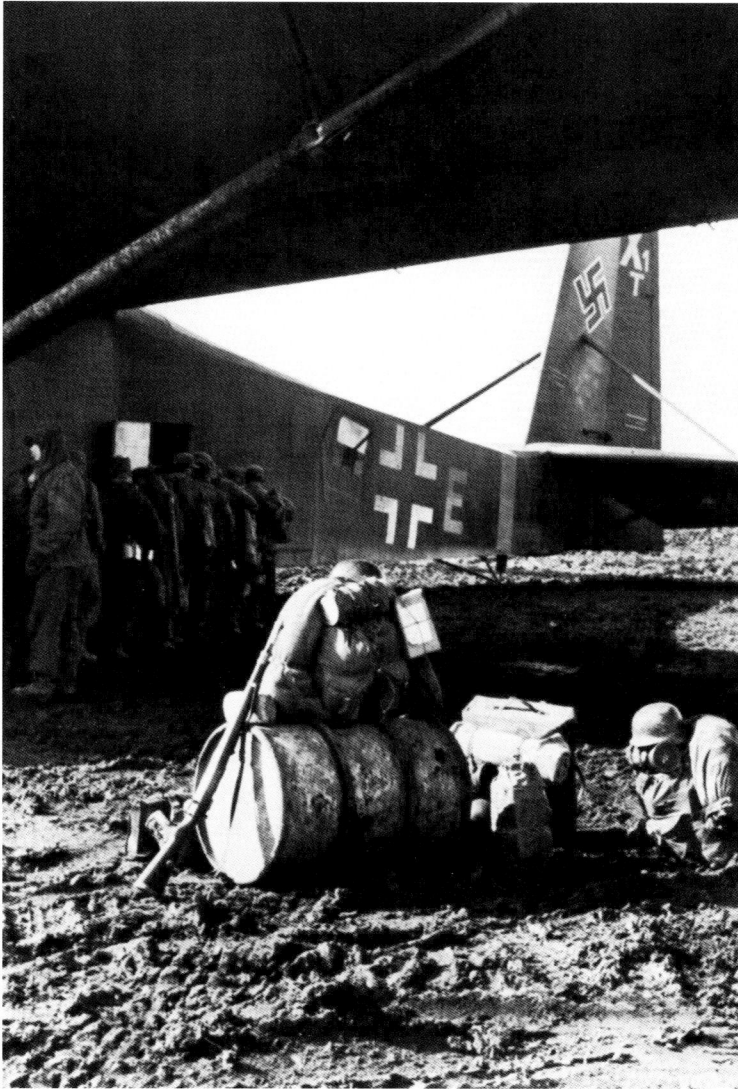

LEFT: When Stab TG 5 was transferred from Italy to the central sector of the Russian Front in October 1943, it organised a large capacity, air transport service behind the German lines to carry heavy goods to all sectors of the Russian Front and, later, bring back wounded. Eventually, this special Grossraum service included the Ju 52/3ms of I./TG 1 and some 30 Me 323s, together with a few Ar 232s, Ju 290s and captured Italian P.108 aircraft but it came to an end in March 1944 when TG 5 transferred to Rumania to assist in missions to and from the Crimea. This photograph shows an Me 323 on a waterlogged airfield on the Eastern Front in late 1943, a time of year when the ground became soft and muddy. Airfields were badly affected, especially where heavily-loaded transport aircraft were operating. Note the tactical marking on the rudder and that only the aircraft letter E has been applied to the fuselage.

ABOVE: This airfield appears to have a hard runway, but at Bobruisk in central Russia, for example, Me 323s created deep ruts and ridges which, when they froze hard in December 1943, caused damage to fighter aircraft using the same airfield. A month later, when the frozen surface began to thaw, a special wooden runway was laid so that the Me 323s could operate without causing further surface damage.

RIGHT: Technical personnel servicing the engines on an Me 323 E-1 of I./TG 5 on the Eastern Front in late 1943. Although the operational fuselage markings have been obscured by mud, the tactical code X1J on the rudder strongly suggests that this may have been C8+EE. Certainly, an aircraft with this marking combination was badly damaged in a forced-landing in March 1944, following which the remains were deliberately destroyed.

LEFT: With all three BMW 132 engines straining, a Ju 52/3m in the Ukraine begins its take-off run.

BELOW AND RIGHT: This Ju 52/3m was being flown from Oslo by Ofw. Anton Dieter of TGr 20 in the winter of 1943/1944 when it ran out of fuel less than three kilometres from its destination at Dresden and crash-landed during a snowstorm. The significance of the small number 8 on the rudder is not fully understood, but may have been associated with the former KGrzbV 108, from which TGr 20 was formed in May 1943; or it may have been the eighth aircraft in its Staffel. The winged barrel badge of KGrzbV 105 on the nose suggests that this machine had earlier served with that unit before being transferred to KGrzbV 108 and thence to TGr 20.

RIGHT: The Go 244, which first appeared in 1942, was a powered version of the Go 242 glider using two Gnome-Rhône 14M engines, large quantities of which had become available following the fall of France in 1940. Although the type equipped KGrzbV 104 and KGrzbV 106, it was found to be underpowered when fully loaded and by the end of 1942 both units had re-equipped with other aircraft. Thereafter, most Go 244s were transferred to training units for airborne troops, although some, as seen here, continued to be used by 7./TG 4 in southern Russia.

BELOW: A snow camouflaged He 111 of Schleppgruppe 4. Little is known about this unit other than it was formed in October 1943 from several independent Lastensegler (Cargo Glider) Staffeln and Lastensegler Kommandos. The Gruppe, believed to have consisted of three Staffeln, was equipped with a number of He 111s and Go 242 gliders and was disbanded in 1944.

BELOW: A winter camouflaged He 111 of 5./KG 4 showing the unit code 5J+GN and with the unit lettering ahead of the Balkenkreuz in small characters. In many instances, KG 4 worked in close co-operation with the Transporters, whether by bombing Soviet anti-aircraft positions during air-drops or by releasing parachute containers. During some sorties, the aircraft performed a dual role, first bombing to suppress enemy ground fire and then releasing their containers.

ABOVE: An He 111 H-20 of KG 27 being loaded with 250 kg supply containers in the winter of 1943/1944. The H-20 was preferred for the transport role as it could carry more containers than the standard bomber versions. It was also found that bomber crews quickly adapted to the role of releasing supply containers because of their experience in bomb aiming.

RIGHT: Another He 111 of KG 27 in Russia showing its winter camouflage.

BELOW: An He 111 H-20, almost certainly of TGr 30, at Ciechanow in northern Poland in early 1944. The H-20 proved particularly successful in the supply role when its useful load and long range was especially appreciated.

Emblem of II./TG 5

LEFT: The extensive exhaust staining on the wings of this Me 323 E-1 of II./TG 5 on the Eastern Front in February 1944 is indicative of extensive operational use. This particular machine was completely destroyed on 24 March 1944, although the cause is not known.

Messerschmitt Me 323 E-1 of 6./TG 5, Eastern Front, February 1944

The operational markings on the fuselage of this aircraft comprised only the letters AP, the unit code C8 being omitted, and indicated that the aircraft was allocated to the Staffelkapitän of 6./TG 5. The badge of II./TG 5 on the forward fuselage featured Baron Münchhausen riding a cannon ball and, in an appropriate reference to the Me 323's six engines, he was depicted being towed by six geese. The camouflage on this machine was the standard 70/71/65 scheme.

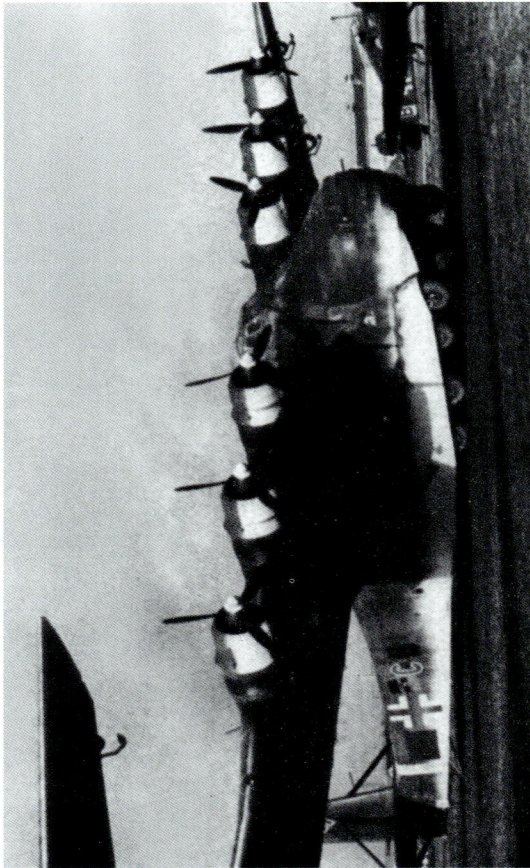

LEFT: The Me 323 E-2 was similar to the E-1 but featured two wing-mounted, electrically-powered turrets, each armed with an MG 151 machine gun. The barrel of one of these weapons may be seen to the rear of the outer starboard engine on this particular machine, C8+CB of Stab I./TG 5. Although shown here on the Eastern Front in 1944, this aircraft may earlier have flown in Italy until the Gruppe transferred to the East in October 1943.

ABOVE: The MG 151 installation is shown more clearly in this view of Luftwaffe aircrew on the Eastern Front removing the snow covers from an Me 323 in early 1944. I./TG 5 was commanded from May 1943 until August 1944 by Major Günther Mauss, who was awarded the German Cross in Gold in the summer of 1943.

Messerschmitt Me 323 E-1 C8+CB of Stab I./TG 5, Russia, 1944

As an aircraft of the Gruppenstab, this machine had its individual aircraft letter in green, outlined in white, and the white spinner tips each had a green ring. The camouflage scheme consisted of a splinter pattern on the uppersurfaces in 70 and 71 with 65 undersurfaces and the undersides of the engine cowlings in yellow. The dark panel of fresh paint aft of the fuselage Balkenkreuz shows where the original large characters of the unit code C8 had been painted out and re-applied in the smaller style.

The Evacuation of the Crimea

Despite their numerous successful rearguard actions, their counter-attacks and the tenacity with which German troops faced the Soviet onslaught in southern Russia, the Germans had nevertheless been forced to withdraw and now held a front which extended from Odessa in the south, which they began to evacuate on 10 April, almost to Brest-Litovsk in the north.

In the Crimea, which had been bypassed by the Soviet advance, the long anticipated attack began on 7 April 1944. By the 10th, the northern front could no longer be held and, in accordance with a contingency plan, German and Rumanian forces began falling back to the fortified area of Sevastopol, from where they were to be evacuated. Despite considerable pressure from the Soviets, who immediately advanced as soon as units abandoned their positions, the withdrawal to the Sevastopol area was accomplished reasonably successfully.

Air transport, which for almost six months had been attempting to assist in the reinforcement of Seventeenth Army, but had been diverted to meet the needs of Eighth and First *Panzer* Armies, among others, was now to redirect every available aircraft to assist in the evacuation of the Crimea. In anticipation of this, a strong force comprising no fewer than 12 separate *Gruppen*, plus two independent *Staffeln* of transport aircraft and gliders, had already been concentrated in eastern Rumania, where the fall of Odessa had resulted in an immediate redistribution of all transport units on the southern sector of the front. Most units, including the previously withdrawn SM.82s of III./TG 1, which now returned to operations, arrived at their new bases from the airfields around Odessa which had previously been used to supply the Crimea.

Units Available for the Air Evacuation of the Crimea

Stab/TG 2 at Galatz controlling

III./TG 1	Calarasi	SM.82
IV./TG 1	Calarasi	Ju 52/3m
III./TG 2	Galati	Ju 52/3m
I./TG 4	Calarasi	Ju 52/3m

Stab/TG 3 at Constanta controlling

I./TG 1	Carli Chici	Ju 52/3m
I./TG 2	Buzau	Ju 52/3m
II./TG 2	Carli Chici	Ju 52/3m
I./TG 3 (One *Staffel*)	Constanta	Ju 52/3m
III./TG 3	Dana Chici	Ju 52/3m

Stab/TG 5 at Zilistea controlling

I./TG 5	Zilistea	Me 323
II./TG 5	Zilistea	Me 323
TGr 30	Buzau	He 111
Schleppgruppe 2	Buzau	He 111, Go 242
		Ju 87, DFS 230
Transportstaffel 5	Zilistea	Ju 290, Piaggio 108

While Seventeenth Army awaited the final signal to begin the evacuations, the smooth evacuation of wounded and non-combat personnel began on the 12th. Still there was every indication that the Seventeenth Army could be saved, but on the same day, and contrary to all expectations, orders from the *Führer* stated that Sevastopol was now to be defended indefinitely. No fighting troops were to be evacuated, but fresh troops were to be flown in to hold the fortress area of Sevastopol.

Transport operations to Sevastopol and the Chersones peninsula began in earnest on 14 April 1944 when ammunition and troops were carried to the Crimea. However, a major Soviet tank assault had been launched on the 12th and the transports could barely keep the troops adequately supplied to resist further attacks. On their return flights, priority was reserved for any troops and equipment not needed for the defence and the enormous numbers of sick and wounded. In order to cope, the crews often took off with their aircraft grossly overloaded, but although all available ambulances and ambulance trains were made ready to receive the wounded at the airfields in Rumania and take them

ABOVE: An important part of transport activity in the East in April 1944 was carried out by the Me 323s of TG 5 based at Kecskemét in central Hungary and at Wiener Neustadt in Austria. Approximately 40 of these giant aircraft were regularly employed on flights to the Rumanian front where their main forward landing ground was Zilistea in Central Rumania. Here, heavy exhaust staining from the Gnome-Rhône 14 M engines is evident in this photograph of C8+EN, an Me 323 of 5./TG 5, photographed while being refuelled in Rumania.

to Army hospitals immediately the aircraft landed, this was not always possible. Sometimes, several thousand wounded were left awaiting transportation, and many of them could not even be brought under cover.

By this time, Soviet air activity over the Crimea and the Black Sea had intensified with attacks on German airfields, ports, convoys and the main defence area. Since there were already too few twin-engined fighters available to protect these targets and the equally few single-engined fighters lacked the necessary bases or range, the transport formations were obliged to fall back on the tactic first employed in the Mediterranean and fly in close formation. When enemy aircraft were sighted, the unit leader fired a green flare to alert his comrades to the threat, and a red flare was the signal for all gunners to open fire at the approaching fighters. At first, this succeeded in forcing the attackers to break off, but towards the end of the evacuation, Russian fighter opposition increased and the transports resorted to flying at night as the Soviets were unable to introduce any night fighters. The number of sorties, however, had to be reduced as the thaw and mud on the landing fields in the Crimea made night landings dangerous.

During this time, the transport crews nevertheless did everything in their power to avoid loading troops for the Crimea but continued to carry in supplies and to fly their return trips dangerously overloaded. On 7 May, the Soviets launched their main assault, and on the night of the 8th, when it became clear that German and Rumanian troops were unable to hold anywhere, Hitler finally agreed to the full-scale evacuation. This came too late, however, and on 9 May the German garrison at Sevastopol surrendered while the remaining troops withdrew into the Chersones peninsula. From this point on, only the wounded were flown out and, during the night of 10 May alone, a thousand were evacuated from one of the last available airfields. It is thought that a total of 21,500 troops were evacuated from the Crimea by air and another 121,000 were taken off by sea before the last German resistance was broken on 12 May and the remaining 26,700 men fell into Soviet hands.

LEFT: An He 111 being connected to a Go 242 glider at Lvov (Lemberg) in Poland in September or October 1943. The unit is almost certainly Verbindungs-kommando (S) 4, which had previously served on the Eastern Front.

LEFT: When it returned to operations later in October 1943, Verbindungs-kommando (S) 4 was redesignated Schleppgruppe 2. At that time, the unit was based at Kirovograd, a major air base in southern Russia, probably the scene of this photograph which shows an He 111 coded F7+BE in the foreground.

RIGHT: A Go 242, probably of Schleppgruppe 4, over Nikolayev in southern Russia in early 1944.

BELOW: Seen in winter conditions is this Go 242 A, coded 4V+2-1, of TG 3. An essential prerequisite for glider operations, especially when the ground troops were on the march, was accurate identification of the landing field. Units were warned that displaying swastika flags and firing coloured flares was not sufficient as the Russians were known to duplicate these signals. In some cases, Russians had appeared in German uniforms and had succeeded in persuading the gliders to land in enemy territory.

LEFT: Soviet PoWs helping to unload a wounded German soldier on a stretcher in January 1944. Soviet soldiers who volunteered to work with the Wehrmacht were known as 'Hiwis', an abbreviation of 'Hilfswillige', or auxiliary volunteer. Although specialised medical Ju 52/3ms existed, they were few in number and, as a rule, wounded were transported by normal Ju 52/3m aircraft. Note the straw inside the fuselage which was provided as insulation.

1943-1945

RIGHT: An Me 323 of Stab II./TG 5 landing at an airfield on the Eastern Front in early 1944. This aircraft is coded C8+AC and carried a tactical code on the rudder. The number of crew in these aircraft varied from eight to ten but nine was the most frequent and consisted of the captain, the pilot, a wireless operator, two mechanics and four air gunners.

LEFT: An He 111 of Schleppgruppe 1 on the Eastern Front, probably in the spring of 1944. A feature of this aircraft is that the last letter of the operational markings has been painted in the Staffel colour rather than the individual aircraft letter. Although unusual, this practice has been observed elsewhere but the reason for such a deviation from standard procedure is not known. Schleppgruppe 1 was formed in November 1943 and remained in existence until May 1945.

RIGHT: An He 111 H of 3./TGr 30 coded S3+LL. While operating in the Crimea between 12 April and 11 May 1944, this Gruppe flew a total of 765 sorties, transported 6,240 troops, 280 tons of supplies and 662 supply containers of the 250 kg size. At the same time, 12,480 wounded and 1,640 troops were evacuated, but six He 111s were lost due to enemy action and another to a technical failure. Casualties amounted to 22 personnel killed, six missing and four wounded.

ABOVE: After being temporarily withdrawn from operations on the Eastern Front due to difficulties in obtaining spares and the type's general unsuitability in winter conditions, the SM.82s of III./TG 1 returned to front-line service during the evacuation of the Crimea in April 1944. This example, IZ+NV of the Gruppe's 11. Staffel, was found at Sevastopol in May, after the Crimea had been retaken by Soviet forces.

BELOW: A Ju 52 of 15./TG 3 on the Eastern Front in the summer of 1944. This Staffel had been formed from 3./KGzbV 172 in May 1943 and continued to use the Gruppe emblem of a pig superimposed on an eight-pointed star painted in the Staffel colour.

1943-1945

ABOVE: An Me 323 of II./TG 5 taking off from an airfield on the Eastern Front in the summer of 1944.

RIGHT: Little is known about this Me 323 of 8./TG 5, probably photographed on the Eastern Front in 1944. Although allocated the operational markings C8+AS, it is possible that the unit code C8 was omitted.

Operation 'Rösselsprung'

From about the middle of July 1943, *Luftwaffenkommando Südost*, which had been formed from parts of X. *Fliegerkorps* in January 1943, began to build up stocks on airfields in Western Greece in anticipation of a possible Allied invasion. The units assigned this task were I./TG 4, which transferred from Jena-Rödigen to Athens-Tatoi, and II./TG 4 which went to Kraljevo in Yugoslavia. During the last two weeks of July, a daily average of some 55 sorties by Ju 52/3ms and four by He 111s with Go 242 gliders took place in this area, the airfields at Salonica, Larissa, Janina and Corfu being considered especially important bases from which to launch counter-attacks should an invasion be attempted. In addition, one of the *Staffeln* of I./TG 4 was at this time equipped with Ju 52/3m floatplanes which flew regularly to Suda, Milos and Rhodes from their bases at Athens-Phaleron.

During August and September 1943, further airfields on Crete, Rhodes, Delvoli, Tirana, Valona and others in western Greece and Albania were similarly stocked and a daily average of some 35 Ju 52/3m lifts was maintained. This German attention to strengthening the islands off the east and west coast of Greece proved fully justified, since the Allies had hoped to take advantage of the surrender of Italy in September and seize the strategically important Aegean island of Rhodes, where the Italian garrison had refused to join the Allies. Although detailed Allied planning for an invasion had commenced, this was postponed in favour of other operations in Italy and the south of France. The idea was not completely abandoned, however, and a similar but smaller operation was proposed in which the Allies would invade some of the lesser Aegean islands. Accordingly, Casteloriso, Cos, Leros, Samos and Stampalia were occupied, but immediate reaction by the Germans soon established their air superiority and was followed by airborne and amphibious forces which recaptured the islands.

The first to be retaken was Cos, where a reinforced *Fallschirmjäger Bataillon* jumped from the aircraft of 6./TG 4 on 3 and 4 October. On 18 October, a platoon of *Fallschirmjäger* was dropped to assist in the capture of Levitha and on the 22nd, more were dropped on Stampalia. Owing to the difficulty of transporting these paratroops back to the mainland, a *Bataillon* from 2. *Fallschirmjäger Division* had to be transferred to Italy at the beginning of November, and paratroops from this division then jumped from about 80 Ju 52/3ms on 12 and 13 November to capture Leros. After the capture of these islands, they had to be garrisoned and supplied and every available aircraft, including Ar 196 floatplanes and Do 24 flying boats, was employed on re-supply operations. Supplies had to be dropped on Leros by He 111s for almost a week after the original parachute attack. Subsequently, the routine tasks undertaken by air transport based in Greece varied little in the next few months.

In January 1944, it was decided to reduce the initial establishment for air transport units from 217 to 192 aircraft in order to match the actual strength in aircraft that could be obtained in the future and to economise on manpower. All *Stab* aircraft were removed and each *Geschwader* was allocated a few light communications types as replacements. At the same time, each *Gruppe* was reorganised on a basis of three *Staffeln*, each with 16 aircraft. The *Flugbetriebskompanie* was dissolved, but a workshop platoon was made part of the *Gruppenstab* and one Servicing Platoon was attached to each *Staffel*.

Also in January 1944, IV./TG 4, previously based at Riga, replaced I./TG 4 at Athens, while II./TG 4 continued to work from Belgrade, Nish, Kraljevo and Athens. Isolated garrisons in the Balkans were re-supplied by a miscellany of Ju 87, Ju 88, W 34, Fw 58 and Fi 156 aircraft, and this allowed the small number of available transport aircraft to continue their routine supply flights from Athens. Losses among these machines were never very heavy, but there was a steady toll of a few aircraft each week due to Allied long-range fighters, while opposing Greek partisan units, which had stepped up their activities against the German occupation forces, also attacked landing grounds.

In mid-February, *Luftwaffe* air transport was largely responsible for the evacuation of a large number of Italian prisoners of war which were taken from Rhodes to Athens. The Italians, required for forced labour in Germany, were packed 25 to each Ju 52/3m for the journey, and after being unloaded, the aircraft flew back to Rhodes and the other Aegean islands with fresh garrison troops. The unit involved in this work is believed to have been II./TG 4, then the mainstay of Aegean transport, with between 35 and 40 Ju 52/3ms.

Meanwhile, in Yugoslavia, resistance to the German occupation had, by early 1944, increased dramatically and large areas of the country were dominated by Communist partisans under Marshal Josip Tito. In order to control this situation, *Oberbefehlshaber Südost* formulated a plan to eliminate Tito by mounting an assault

Marshal Josip Tito, President of the National Liberation committee, seen here with his bodyguard, was to have been eliminated in a German assault against his headquarters carried out under the code-name Operation 'Rösselsprung'.

against his mountain stronghold. Several earlier attempts to either kill or capture the partisan leader had failed but had compelled him to relocate his headquarters from Jajce to near the small town of Drvar in Bosnia. From various intelligence sources and wireless intercepts, the precise location of the headquarters was believed to be a cave some five kilometres from the centre of Drvar.

Control of the operation, code-named '*Rösselsprung*' (Knight's Move) was allocated to XV. *Gebirgsarmeekorps* and was to take place at the end of May. The plan called for various battle units of the German and Croat Armies, assisted by the 7. *Waffen-SS Division 'Prinz Eugen'*, to advance on Tito's headquarters. At the same time, an airborne assault was to be mounted by 340 *Luftwaffe* glider troops and a further 314 parachute troops which included men from the little-known *SS-Fallschirmjäger Bataillon 500*. The *Luftwaffe* was to provide air support on and over the landing ground and assembled a force of more than 130 gliders, of which the majority were DFS 230s, to transport the airborne troops to the target area. These and the various towing aircraft, which comprised a mixture of Hs 126s, He 46s, Ju 87s, He 111s and Avia B 534s, were provided by *Schleppgruppe* 1 and II. and III./LLG 1. The *SS* parachute troops were to be dropped by some 40 Ju 52/3ms of II./TG 4, possibly reinforced with additional machines and crews from II./TG 2.

ABOVE: By 1943 the demand for Ju 52/3m aircraft had increased to the point where it seemed wasteful to tie up a large number of these useful aircraft in glider towing units, especially as there was little possibility of major airborne operations in the future. Moreover, as the DFS 230 glider could be towed by less powerful and obsolescent types, the Ju 52/3ms were withdrawn for use by the Transportgruppen and replaced by the Do 17, Hs 126, Avia 534, Fw 44, He 46 and Ju 87. This photograph of a DFS 230 and an elderly Ju 87 B of II. or III./LLG 1, was taken in the Balkans in 1944. Subsequently, the strength of the Luftlandegeschwader gradually declined until September 1944 when LLG 1 and LLG 2 were disbanded. The remaining aircraft were used to reinforce local reconnaissance units, and the gliders were stored until January 1945 when they were extensively employed on the Eastern Front.

'*Rösselsprung*' was launched at first light on the morning of 25 May, and although the paratroops and most of the gliders succeeded in landing in their assigned areas, the partisans quickly recovered from their surprise and mounted fierce opposition. Similarly, the ground advance, which was to link up and relieve the air-landed forces, also met with strong opposition and was delayed. Nevertheless, the *SS* stormed Tito's cave but the defenders had been able to hold the narrow mountain approaches long enough for Tito to escape via a secret exit. Unaware that Tito had already fled, the Ju 52/3ms of II./TG 4 dropped a second wave of parachute troops into the area around midday and flew further supply sorties during the night of the 25th. This allowed the air-landed forces in Drvar and its surroundings to hold out against partisan opposition until the first relief troops reached them at midday on the 26th. When German troops finally broke through to Tito's cave, they discovered only his Jeep and his uniform jacket.

BELOW: An example of an He 46, as used by LLG 1, showing the Geschwader badge.

BELOW: A DFS 230 glider of LLG 1 with one of the unit's Do 17s in the background.

RIGHT: A formation of Ju 52/3ms towing DFS 230 gliders.

BELOW: In the foreground of this photograph of 'Rösselsprung' in progress is a DFS 230 glider of LLG 1 while, in the background, the Ju 52/3ms of II./TG 4 arrive with more Fallschirmjäger. As from 1942, and because of the heavy casualties sustained in Crete when the paratroopers could not reach their weapons containers, paratroops received regular training in jumping with weapons. This proved very successful and from then on, the paratroops jumped carrying pistols and either a machine pistol, rifle, light machine gun, boxes of ammunition for machine guns and medium mortars, machine gun stands, or short entrenching tools. Medium mortar tubes, mortar base plates and radio sets were dropped by auxiliary parachutes attached to each paratrooper.

LEFT: The DFS 230 glider landings at Drvar were followed by Fallschirmjäger jumping from the Ju 52/3ms of II./TG 4.

ABOVE LEFT: One of the DFS 230 troop gliders used during Unternehmen 'Rösselsprung' in June 1944. This example carries the fuselage code H4+4-39 and belonged to 7./LLG 1.

ABOVE RIGHT: German troops displaying Tito's uniform jacket.

The Aegean and the Balkans

In June, the activity of transport units in the Mediterranean declined considerably, particularly during the second half of the month, due to the opening of the front in Normandy on 6 June which necessitated diverting aircraft to supplement requirements in northern France and Germany. Accordingly, I., II. and III./TG 1, I. and II./TG 2, I. and II./TG 3 and I./TG 4 were all withdrawn from the Balkans, while the activities of TG 5 and the Ju 290s of *LTStaffel* 5 declined. Conversely, Ju 52/3ms of 14./TG 3 appeared in the Balkans, 15./TG 3 appeared in Italy and *Transport Staffel/ I. Fliegerkorps* with mixed transport and communications types appeared in Rumania.

On 24 August 1944, *OKW* ordered the evacuation of Crete, the Aegean islands, and later the whole of the Balkan Peninsula. The air evacuation involved II./TG 4 and IV./TG 1, two of the most experienced Ju 52/3m units, then based on airfields at Athens. As both units were operationally tired and serviceability was low, they were reinforced by the Ju 52/3m floatplanes of *LTStaffel (See)* 1 and *LTStaffel (See)* 3 operating from Athens-Phaleron and by the similarly equipped I./TG 4. However, this extra transport capacity was quickly offset by the high losses caused by Allied heavy bombing of the Athens and Phaleron airfields where some 80 Ju 52/3ms of II./TG 4 and IV./TG 1 were destroyed. To compensate for these losses, further Ju 52/3ms were allocated from disbanded *Gruppen* and from industry and workshops in Germany. Also employed were the Ju 290 and Piaggio 108 heavy transport aircraft of *LTStaffel* 5, and in order to extend air transport from Athens to Salonika in Greece and thence to Belgrade in Yugoslavia, a number of He 111s from KG 27 and KG 4 were brought up to Athens. Due to Allied fighter patrols, most air transport sorties between Crete and Athens were flown under cover of darkness.

Although it was not possible in the available time to evacuate all the 60,000 men who were garrisoned in the Aegean, the air and sea transport at hand succeeded in bringing back two-thirds to mainland Greece. The remainder continued to hold Rhodes, Leros, Kos, Tilos, Crete and Lilos and remained there until the end of the war.

When British forces landed in Greece and entered Athens on 14 October 1944, *Luftwaffe* air transport units were in the process of retiring to the Salonika area in northern Greece. A shortage of fuel caused serious delays to aircraft as well as motor transport withdrawing towards the Agram area, but it is estimated that in the final phase of the evacuations in Greece and the Balkans in September and October, at least 30,000 men and 1,200 tons of equipment were transported, at least part of the way, by air.

BELOW: A formation of Ju 52/3ms somewhere over Italy or Greece. Up until June 1944, a sizeable transport force was maintained in Greece and in Italy, but the need to withdraw troops before they were cut off by Soviet advances in southern Russia and Rumania, coupled with the Allied landings in Normandy in June, led to a decline in transport activity as units were diverted elsewhere.

LEFT AND BELOW: By mid-May 1944, Germany was faced with Soviet offensives all along the Eastern Front, an Allied offensive from the Anzio beachhead in Italy and the threat of an Allied invasion in the West. There was also a complicated supply situation in Greece that became worse as the forces from the south Russian Front moved westward through Rumania. These two photographs show G6+DP, a Ju 52/3m of 7./TG 4 shortly before a flight to Athens. Note the open engine cowling and the tactical code II7D in yellow on the rudder, the Roman II indicating the Gruppe and the 7 the Staffel. Some units employed such identification markings until late in the war, and in January 1945, other aircraft of TG 4, one with the code II5N of 5. Staffel and another marked ISC of Stab, I. Gruppe, were found at Tatoi and Salonika respectively. Another machine, 1Z+RX of 13./TG 1, found at Eleusis at the same time, had the rudder code D1R.

BELOW: In December 1943, Ju 52/3m floatplanes were operated in the Eastern Mediterranean and Balkans with a floatplane Staffel of TG 4, to which LTSta (See) 1 was attached. Later, LTSta (See) 1 was absorbed into TG 4 and became its 17. Staffel. However, as TG 4 is known to have used Roman numerals in the tactical code to indicate the Gruppe, it would seem that even after the redesignation, some aircraft of 17./TG 4 may have been attached to I./TG 4.

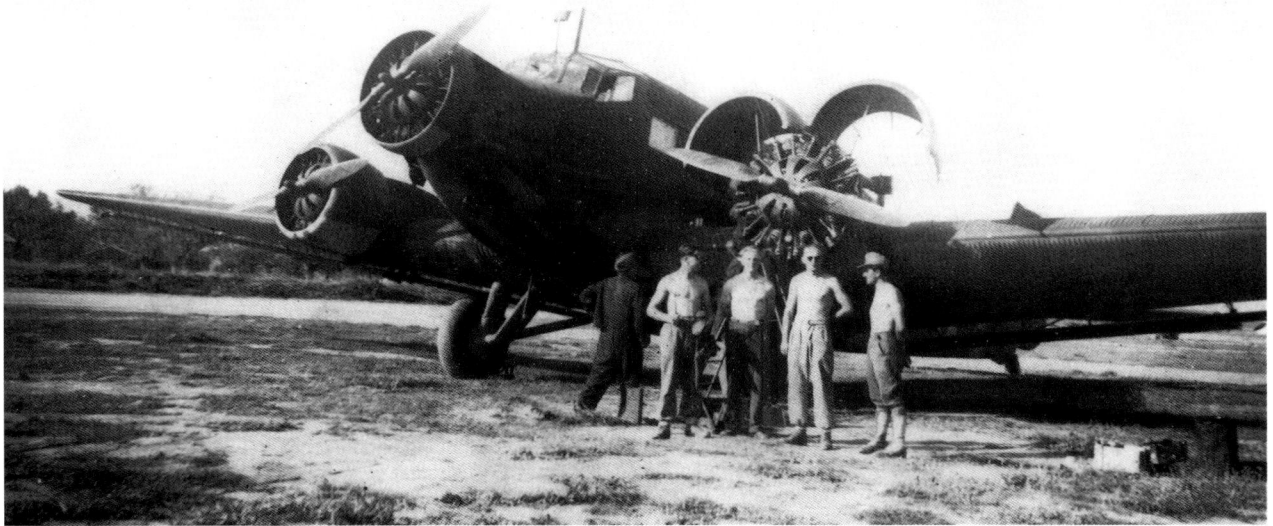

1943-1945

RIGHT: The tactical code on the rudder of this machine is obscured by the open window of the aircraft from which the photograph was taken, but it is almost certainly ISH. Although probably an aircraft of 17./TG 4, the Roman numeral on the rudder suggests this was again a machine operating with I./TG 4. Note the effect of the salt water corrosion on the floats where the paintwork below the waterline has been stripped away.

ABOVE: A Ju 52/3m floatplane over the Aegean. In April 1944, the Balkans were reinforced and the Ju 52/3m floatplanes based at Salonika-Mikra were very busy visiting the Aegean islands of Lemnos, Leros, Mytilene and Paros. By May, some crews were flying twice daily as up to 20 sorties per day were being made, mainly between Phaleron and the Aegean islands. This aircraft had the operational identification 8A+EJ and carried the tactical code W1E on the rudder.

RIGHT: These Ju 52/3m floatplanes with the markings 8A+AJ and 8A+LJ were employed in the operations to evacuate troops from islands in the Aegean in September 1944. Although these machines still carry the unit code of LT Staffel (See) 1, they are believed to have been operating under the control of TG 4 when photographed, or may possibly have already been absorbed as that unit's 17. Staffel.

The Ju 52/3m4e, g5e, g8e, g10e and g14e could all be fitted with floats under the general designation Ju 52/3m Wasser, or Ju 52/3m See, and were specifically designed to allow the wheeled undercarriage to be easily exchanged for floats. These aircraft proved useful for operations in the Aegean and eastern Mediterranean where they operated for some months. This Ju 52/3m floatplane was photographed (LEFT) taking off in the Aegean, probably in late May 1943, although it still carries the winter scheme applied during previous service in southern Russia. Although the fuselage code 1Z+MN indicates the machine had earlier served with 5./KGzbV 1, recently redesignated 5./TG 1, the tactical code W1K on the rudder indicates that, when photographed, it was serving with LT Staffel (See) 1. The aircraft later sank at Athens-Phaleron following a landing accident but, as shown (RIGHT), was salvaged from the sea on 1 June 1943.

Junkers Ju 52/3m of LT Staffel (See) 1, Aegean, June 1943

Although operating in the Aegean, the standard 70/71 uppersurfaces on this machine were still covered in a temporary white winter finish as the aircraft had recently transferred from the Eastern Front. It is presumed, therefore, that as the machine might have been expected to return at any time to its operational area in southern Russia, it probably retained the yellow theatre markings under the wingtips. The undersurfaces were 65 and the standard yellow recognition markings appeared under the engine cowlings. Note that the profile depicts the machine after the tactical code W1K had been added to the rudder.

Luftwaffe Transport during the Invasion of France and North-West Europe

By early 1944, it had become obvious to *OKW* that the Allies in the West would almost certainly attempt an invasion that year. In preparation for this, Allied daylight bombing policy had concentrated on eliminating the *Luftwaffe's* fighter force, whether in the factories where they were being manufactured or in aerial combat. Fighter losses increased daily, and in response to this critical situation, a so-called *Jägerstab* was established to disperse the aircraft industry and increase fighter production. This, however, was only possible by implementing corresponding reductions in the production of other aircraft types, and although bomber production was continued in order to meet Hitler's insistence on retaliation, production of training, communications and transport aircraft was necessarily reduced. Thus, whereas in 1943, 1,028 transport aircraft had been produced, of which 887 were Ju 52/3ms, total production during 1944 dropped to 443, of which 379 were Ju 52/3ms.

As for meeting the anticipated invasion itself, plans were organised under a series of *Drohende Gefahr* (State of Emergency) schemes, but not knowing where the Allied landing would take place, many plans had to be drawn up to meet emergencies which might occur anywhere from Norway to the South of France. With regard to air transport, there was not a great deal that could be done, for by the spring of 1944 the transport fleet was already so heavily committed elsewhere, mainly in the East, that there were few aircraft which could be spared. If an Allied landing was attempted in Norway, for example, it was originally the German intention to employ the Ju 87s and DFS 230s of 8./LLG 1, and this *Staffel* had in fact toured Norway the previous summer to demonstrate the usefulness of gliders for air transport. However, by March, the *Staffel* was committed in

the Balkans and it was agreed instead that *Lufttransportstaffel* 5 with Piaggio 108 heavy transports would be a more satisfactory reinforcement should a state of emergency develop in the far north.

More positive steps were taken with regard to certain *Gruppen* which were to be re-fitted and held in Germany and Czechoslovakia as reserves against a state of emergency. Consequently, I./TG 1, II./TG 3, I./TG 4 and III./TG 4 were withdrawn from the south Russian Front at the end of May 1944 and, at the same time, a Ju 52/3m *Luftverkehrsgruppe (Mot.)* was called up from *Lufthansa* and from communications units within Germany and was stationed at Calau. More surprisingly, the parachute and supply-dropping unit TGr 30, equipped with He 111s, was also withdrawn from the front in southern Russia in May and sent to Kaufbeuren where it was due to be disbanded at the beginning of June.

When the Allied landings began in Normandy on the night of 5/6 June 1944, the first task of air transport was to move fighter and bomber units up to their new operational airfields in France while at the same time transferring training units away from the operational area. Great reliance was therefore placed upon the air transport units, but of the units held in reserve and due to reinforce *Luftflotte* 3 when the invasion took place, I./TG 1 had already been assigned to *Luftflotte* 6 on the Russian Front, II./TG 3 and I./TG 4 were still in Germany, and III./TG 4 was engaged in parachute training. Consequently, although other transport units arrived later in June, the *Luftverkehrsgruppe (Mot.)* was the only *Gruppe* actually allocated to *Luftflotte* 3 in France when the Allies landed.

Next in importance was ensuring that the operational units were adequately supplied with ammunition and fuel. Prior to the invasion, stocks of bombs, ammunition and fuel had been built up in France sufficient for about a month of operations by fighter-bomber and bomber aircraft, so while no particular supply difficulties were encountered, the Allies had, as part of their pre-invasion preparations, practically destroyed all rail communications in France. Any supplies had, therefore, to be brought from the dumps to the

ABOVE: In the summer of 1943, the Ju 87s and DFS 230s of 8./LLG 1 toured Norway to demonstrate the usefulness of gliders, should an Allied landing be attempted there. This photograph was probably taken at that time and shows a DFS 230 being prepared at Lister.

BELOW: Photographed a few months before the Allied invasion in France, this SM.82 apparently crash-landed at Celle on 11 April 1944. The machine was coded 4V+AU and belonged to 10./TG 3.

operational units by road or by air. Although almost the entire German home defence force, comprising 15 fighter *Gruppen* with some 300 aircraft, had flown in from Germany by 10 June, many of which were operating as fighter-bombers, it was the bomber units which mainly required supplying.

Quite distinct from the transport operations flown in support of units moving base and to ensure they were adequately supplied, further sorties were soon being flown to troops which had become separated from their sources of supply due to Allied ground actions. Sorties of this nature were assigned to *Luftverkehrsgruppe (Mot.)* and TGr 30, the earlier plan to disband this latter *Gruppe* having been cancelled as soon as the *Drohende Gefahr* materialised. On the evening of 8 June, the three *Staffeln* of TGr 30 moved to the airfields at Metz, Diedenhofen and Trier where the aircraft were dispersed and carefully camouflaged to conceal them from the large number of Allied fighters which roamed the area almost without interruption. The *Gruppe's* main take-off base, however, was at Orly near Paris, and the aircraft and crews required to take part in operations flew there under cover of darkness.

Orly was well stocked with supply containers, and although the runway had been heavily damaged, it was quickly repaired so that TGr 30 was able to fly its first operation on the Invasion Front on the night of 19/20 June 1944. By this time, the Allies had broken out of their beachhead and had trapped German forces at Cherbourg in the Cotentin Peninsula. The task was to air-drop 50 tons of armour-piercing ammunition and was assigned to 35 of the *Gruppe's* He 111s. The first aircraft took off at 2130 hrs, with the rest following at three-minute intervals, each crew flying individually and at low level to the drop area just outside Cherbourg. The drop area was well marked, the supplies were delivered accurately, and with all but one aircraft returning to the dispersal airfields, the operation was judged a success.

Between 20 and 30 June, TGr 30 flew a total of 188 tons of supplies to Cherbourg, and similar operations were subsequently carried out to St. Malo and the Cap de la Hague, mainly by aircraft carrying weapons and infantry ammunition. All sorties were flown at night, with supplies being dropped from the air as it was not possible for the aircraft to land.

Further reinforcements for the air transport units on the Invasion Front arrived in August when the SM.82s of TG 1 were transferred to Niedermendig, and soon afterwards, I./TG 2 was ordered to take over the aircraft of *Luftverkehrsgruppe (Mot.)* and establish itself at Mainz-Finthen. Later that month, after US forces had overrun Brittany and advanced southwards, the long-term air supply began to pockets of German resistance holding out at Brest, St. Nazaire, the Channel Islands, La Rochelle and Lorient, for which task TGr 30 was reinforced by II. and III./KG 53. Having finally been released from its duties in Germany, III./TG 3 arrived at Strasbourg, the transit station for all supplies flown into France, on 1 September.

In the meantime, I./LLG 1, with Do 17s and DFS 230 gliders, undertook supply flights to small German forces engaged in suppressing French Resistance uprisings. These had begun during the second half of May and coincided with an increase in Resistance activity prior to the invasion, but in central and south-eastern France they continued with great intensity until mid-August. Some of the DFS 230s were therefore used by the so-called '*Geschwader Bongart*' during an action in July 1944 when some 10,000 French partisans were surrounded by *Fallschirmjäger* and mountain troops from the Army's 157th Reserve Division which landed on the Vercors Plateau, south of Grenoble, and inflicted heavy losses in an action conducted with great brutality.

ABOVE: One of the Allied beaches shortly after the D-Day landings in June 1944. When the landings took place, few transport aircraft could be spared as they were heavily committed elsewhere, predominantly in the East. The air transport role was therefore at first mainly undertaken by Luftverkehrsgruppe (Mot.) and TGr 30 until, during the second half of June, aircraft in the Mediterranean were diverted to supplement requirements in northern France and Germany. The units transferred included I., II. and III./TG 1, I. and II./TG 2, I. and II./TG 3 and I./TG 4.

BELOW: Two examples of the supply containers carried by the He 111 when operating in the transport role. The soldier standing on the right gives an indication of scale.

As a result of the *Luftwaffe's* increased operational activity since D-Day and the effects of the Allied air offensive against oil production plants, supplies of fuel had run so low that it had been necessary to break into *OKW's* strategic reserves of aviation fuel. By July, acute difficulties were experienced with supply and on the 6th, Göring ordered that drastic economy was absolutely essential. All liaison travel and communications flights were to be reduced and transport flights limited strictly to operational requirements and the supply of the fighting forces. By August, this fuel shortage, together with the reduced production of transport aircraft, resulted in severe economies being introduced which stripped the air transport units of everything deemed unnecessary. Units were disbanded, but with pilots being encouraged to retrain as fighter pilots for the Defence of the Reich and other aircrew being drafted into the Parachute Army, there was also the beginning of a manpower shortage.

Towards the middle of September, the demands for air supply increased, and in addition to the garrisons already mentioned above, Dunkirk, Calais, Cap Gris Nez, Royon and the Gironde were all supplied or partly supplied. Most flights were made by the He 111s of TGr 30, now operating from Zellhausen and other airfields in the Frankfurt area. The low scale of losses allowed the *Gruppe* to maintain an establishment of ten aircraft and crews per *Staffel* without difficulty, average serviceability being about seven aircraft per *Staffel*. Originally, *Staffel* strength had been 16 aircraft and crews, but this was found to be too unwieldy and by June 1944 the establishment had been fixed at ten.

On account of Allied fighter and anti-aircraft opposition, operations by TGr 30 continued to be carried out at night, the aircraft crossing the front line at a height of about 18,000 metres, which was sufficient to put them beyond the range of Allied infantry and light anti-aircraft fire. Once beyond the front line, however, the rest of the flight was flown at low level, usually under 300 metres, in order to avoid radar detection, and complete W/T and R/T silence was maintained. Landing to unload supplies was possible at Guernsey and Jersey in the Channel Islands, St. Nazaire, La Rochelle and the Gironde but supplies for Dunkirk and Lorient were air-dropped.

At this time, TGr 30 was equipped with the He 111 H-16 and the more specialised H-20. As fitted for use by TGr 30, the space normally occupied by the bomb bay in the H-16 was equipped with extra fuel tanks to increase the aircraft's range while the cargo was carried in supply containers mounted on racks attached to the underside of the centre section. The H-20 was similar, but although it, too, could carry externally-mounted supply containers, it could also be fitted to carry up to 16 paratroops or supplies within the fuselage. Both types proved extremely useful, but as their numbers diminished, so more of the older and less efficient He 111 H-16s were pressed into service, some arriving from the bomber *Geschwader* KG 53.

The nature of the loads carried by TGr 30 varied from special ammunition, military equipment, and specialised naval items, to mail and edible provisions, although a bulk supply of food was not necessary. At operational briefings, a suggested course was always given although crews were allowed considerable latitude in this matter and, if they wished, could fly a different course. Observers in the unit were all highly experienced, and good navigation, which was solely by dead reckoning, was essential for the hazardous type of work in which the unit was engaged. Navigational errors could prove fatal, and some aircraft accidentally flew into hillsides or other obstacles.

The aircraft of TGr 30 usually took off at dusk in order to fly in darkness when over hostile territory. Despite the risk of anti-aircraft fire, the entire outward and return flights were made at heights varying from tree-top level to a maximum of 275 metres in order to avoid detection and, particularly, night fighters which the crews believed posed the greatest danger. In fact, most aircraft were shot down by anti-aircraft guns, although losses due to enemy action remained on a very moderate scale. More serious was the fact that very often aircraft set out on supply flights but were unable to identify the landing grounds or dropping zones. These areas should have been marked with pre-arranged ground lights which were normally laid out in geometric patterns and changed for each operation, but failure on the part of the reception party to adhere to the correct signals sometimes resulted in crews being unable to find the pre-arranged area. The aircraft therefore had to return with their loads intact, and it was estimated that, in addition to precious fuel, a third of the total effort was wasted in such failed operations.

Equally serious were the consequences of failing to maintain low altitude, as shown by an incident which occurred on 25 September.

An He 111 H-20 of TGr 30 in flight. After the Allied invasion in Normandy in June 1944, the main task of this unit was the delivery of supplies to fortresses on the French coast which had been bypassed by the Allies, some of which held out until May 1945. An unusual feature of this photograph is that, although some sorties began in twilight in order that the aircraft was over its target in total darkness, aircraft rarely flew together, and even when several aircraft were briefed to supply the same area, they took off and made their way to the target alone. A number of TGr 30's aircraft were fitted with towing attachments, as seen on this machine, and all aircraft of the Gruppe were equipped with FuG 10, FuG 101 radio altimeters and FuG 6.

At 0230 hrs, an He 111 H-20 of 3./TGr 30 coded S3+NK took off from Zellhausen to drop ammunition and supplies to German forces at Calais. However, the crew later became lost and, after flying around for about an hour, they climbed to 3,000 m in order to establish their position. Almost immediately, the *Bordfunker* sighted an Allied night fighter, and although the pilot took evasive action by diving to port, the night fighter opened fire and scored hits. The strikes killed the *Bordfunker* and set the starboard engine on fire, at which point the pilot promptly baled out. The observer, who had never flown the aircraft before, took over the controls and made a good belly-landing 10 km north-west of Liege, where the crew, and later the pilot who had baled out, were taken prisoner.

On 1 October 1944, many of the old and experienced transport units and organisations were dissolved in order to release some 8,000 personnel required by the Army to compensate for infantry losses. In the ensuing weed-out, the staffs of the *Generalkommando*/XIV. *Fliegerkorps* and *Transportführer* 1 and 2 were disbanded, and other formations which disappeared from the strength of the transport units included all *Geschwaderstäbe*, the Me 323s of TG 5, two independent *Transportfliegerstaffeln* and no fewer than eight other *Transportgruppen*.

Thus, an additional burden was placed upon the already hard-pressed TGr 30, and in late October, in a sudden escalation of losses, four He 111s of 2. *Staffel* were shot down by anti-aircraft fire while taking supplies to Dunkirk, one on the night of the 22nd and the other three on the 26th. For the latter operation, five He 111s, mostly H-20s of 1., 2. and 3./TGr 30, took off independently from their respective bases in the Frankfurt area. The pilot of one of the Heinkels, coded S3+DL, made his way to the target area at heights varying between 92 and 152 metres, and after passing over Dunkirk, he banked his machine over the area preparatory to releasing the containers. At that moment, he and the observer saw what they thought was another aircraft going down in flames and decided to circle to the east. Soon afterwards, their aircraft was caught by searchlights and almost immediately hit in the fuselage by light anti-aircraft fire. With the port engine on fire, the fuselage well alight and the *Bordmechanic* and air-gunner believed to be seriously wounded, the containers were jettisoned and the pilot gave the order to bale out. The pilot left first followed by the observer, and although both were captured, the pilot remained at large for three days before he was taken prisoner near Ghent. All other members of the crew perished in the crash.

As mentioned previously, a shortage of fuel on the Invasion Front had first arisen in early July, although the prime contributing factor at that time was distribution rather than production. Nevertheless, by August 1944 the shortage had caused the intermittent curtailment of operations by all branches of the *Luftwaffe*, and by November, had worsened to the point where further economies were called for and necessitated more restrictions being imposed on transport flights. On 18 November, transport flights other than to the Channel Islands and besieged fortresses were ordered to be discontinued immediately and only resumed by special order. In effect, this confined the supply effort to the sorties being flown by TGr 30 which, at that time, still had between 30 and 35 aircraft and crews, divided more or less equally between the three *Staffeln*. The *Gruppe's* activity, however, was on a low scale and most operations were flown with small numbers of aircraft, although small emergency supply-dropping operations were also organised from time to time. Typical of these were the operations flown to supply a pocket of troops of *General* Gustav von Zangen's Fifteenth Army holding the Scheldt Estuary, so denying the Allies the vital supply port of Antwerp.

Walter Hornung had a long career with the Luftwaffe's air transport units and was Kommandeur of TGr. 30 in the months following the Normandy invasion. Previously, after serving as a Hauptmann and Staffelkapitän of 4./KGzbV 400, he became a Major and was Staffelkapitän of 4./KGzbV 'Wittstock' when awarded the German Cross in Gold in January 1942. For a brief period in June 1944 he was Kommandeur of III./TG 2, during which time he was awarded the Ritterkreuz on 9 June. He then led TGr 30 and, post-war, served in the Bundesluftwaffe.

'Autumn Mist'

In the daring and imaginative German counter-attack in the Ardennes, planned under the code-name *'Wacht am Rhein'*, Hitler intended to strike through Luxembourg and Belgium and retake Antwerp. The whole operation was perilous, but if successful would disrupt Allied supplies and separate the Americans from the British and Canadians, thus affording German forces the opportunity to destroy the Allied armies piecemeal. The attack, launched under the new code-name *'Herbstnebel'*, or 'Autumn Mist', was planned to open on 16 December. A critical role was to be performed by the Sixth *SS Panzer* Army which was to advance towards Liege and thence on towards Antwerp and the Albert canal. To support Sixth *SS Panzer* Army in the first phase of its drive, parachute troops were to be dropped behind the American lines, specifically on an important multiple road junction on the Eupen to Malmedy road, where they would form a blocking position on Sixth *SS Panzer* Army's right flank. They were then to prevent US forces from the north interfering with the advance and were to remain in position until relieved by forward elements of the 12. *SS Panzer* Division.

The parachute operation, code-named *'Stosser'* and originally planned for the early morning of 15 December, was placed under the command of *Oberst Freiherr* Friedrich-August von der Heydte, who had taken part in all the *Luftwaffe's* major parachute operations and had been Operations Officer to the 2. *Fallschirmjäger Division* in Italy in 1943. More recently, he had commanded *Fallschirmjäger Regiment* 6 in Holland and had just begun forming a *Fallschirmjäger* battle training school.

Two Ju 52/3m *Gruppen* – II./TG 3 under *Major* Otto Baumann and a composite group under *Major* Hans Brambach – with a total of some 67 aircraft, were allocated to the operation, together with four *Fallschirmjäger* light infantry companies, one heavy weapons company, plus one signals and one supply platoon. The total complement, however, comprised only 800 men and, although staffed by experienced instructors from 1. *Fallschirmjäger Schule* at Stendal, the tasks to be accomplished demanded a much larger force. Other flaws in the operation, planning for which only commenced on 8 December, related to the Ju 52/3m crews. Only half of them had previous operational experience, two thirds of the pilots had never dropped paratroops before, and although the operation was to commence at 03.00 hrs local time, a third of the crews had no blind-flying experience. As if this was not enough to jeopardise the operation from the outset, the *Fallschirmjäger*, some of whom had not previously jumped from an aeroplane, had so heavily armed themselves with as many weapons as possible, that the safe take-off weight of each aircraft was exceeded. The unsuspecting pilots therefore had difficulty in getting their machines off the ground and, indeed, one machine from II./TG 3 ran into a group of trees while trying to take off. Miraculously, no one was hurt.

To compensate for the Ju 52/3m crews' lack of experience, it was decided that the formation of transports would be guided to the drop area by a marker *Gruppe* equipped with Ju 88 S aircraft. At almost the last moment, however, the *Gruppe* was unable to carry out the operation and the task was assigned instead to NSG 20, a night ground-attack unit equipped with Fw 190s. The objective was to release flares over a crossroads situated in the centre of a clear area in an otherwise remote wooded region.

After various delays, the operation was finally launched in the early hours of 17 December, and as a diversion to draw enemy fire, dummy paratroops were dropped by Ju 88s. The *Kommandeur* of NSG 20, *Major* Kurt Dahlmann, led the operation to mark the target for the para-drop using the 'Egon' guidance method of radar control. Although the target was completely obscured by cloud cover down to 200 metres, the flares were released at 1,400 metres under 'Egon' control. Descending through the clouds to observe the results, Dahlmann was delighted to see that, despite a strong wind, the flares were suspended precisely over the road junction.

The transports were meanwhile approaching the target area in a loose stream but, to aid the pilots who lacked blind-flying experience, they were flying with their aircraft navigation lights on. Consequently, at least two aircraft were shot down by night fighters before they reached the drop zone, and more were lost on their return flight. Another eight aircraft became lost and ran into heavy enemy anti-aircraft fire, while the dispatchers in other aircraft mistook the gun flashes and fires on the ground for the expected signals and ordered their men to jump over the wrong area. Due to the inaccurate weather forecasts and the overloading of the aircraft, other machines failed to maintain the correct speed in the high winds, and although they arrived over the correct target area, the flares had already burned out. Yet other aircraft released about 200 men some 80 kilometres from the drop zone.

The high wind speed also caused further difficulties and resulted in the *Fallschirmjäger* being scattered and half of them receiving injuries as they crashed through trees or were dragged over the ground by their parachutes. Weapons and equipment containers were also widely dispersed and damaged in the drop, no medical gear could be located, none of the three W/T sets could be made to function and only one medium mortar could be saved. Nevertheless, by the evening of the 17th, some 300 *Fallschirmjäger* had regrouped under von der Heydte and although critically short of food and ammunition, managed to hold out for three days. During this time they sabotaged motor traffic, held up lorries and staff cars, captured a number of US troops and succeeded in intercepting various American staff orders and dispatches. This resulted in the acquisition of some valuable intelligence but which, unfortunately, could not be communicated to 6. *Panzer* Army because of the loss of the radios.

The unit to which this Ju 52/3m belonged is not known, although the style of winter camouflage would strongly indicate TG 3, one of the units which took part in Operation 'Stosser' in the Ardennes. Note the black undersurfaces and the unidentified badge on the nose.

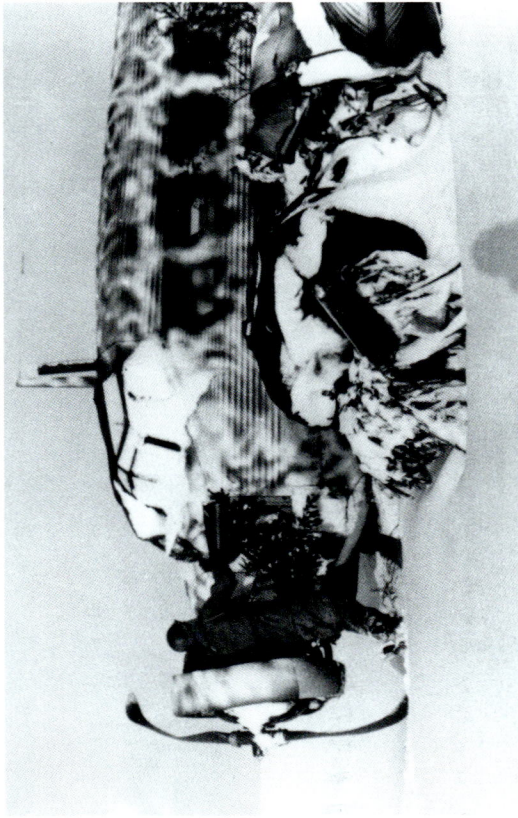

ABOVE LEFT: This Ju 53/3m of 6./TG 3, shown being examined by US troops, is one of two such aircraft which landed close to a German field hospital near Asselborn in northern Luxembourg on 22 January 1945. Almost certainly this aircraft had earlier been involved in Operation 'Stosser', which took place in the early morning of 17 December 1944 and in which two Ju 52/3m Gruppen, II./TG 3 and III./TG 4, had taken part.

ABOVE RIGHT: This is the other Ju 52/3m which landed at Asselborn on 22 January 1945. It had a slightly different form of winter camouflage to that on 4V+BP but was also fitted with flame dampers for night operations and a de-icing system.

Junkers Ju 52/3m 4V+BP of 6./TG 3, January 1945

For a winter camouflage, this aircraft, W.Nr. 7279, has received a meandering overspray of white over the green 70/71 splinter pattern uppersurfaces. The undersurfaces were 65 with all of the area outboard of the wing Balkenkreuz in yellow, and the operational markings 4V+BP on the fuselage were in black with the individual aircraft letter 'B' outlined in white. Note the flame dampers fitted to the exhausts, the de-icing duct leading from the engine nacelle to the uncorrugated wing leading edge and the antenna for the FuG 101 radio altimeter under the port wing.

Attempts to re-supply the paratroops were carried out by some 20 He 111s of TGr 30 which dropped supplies on the nights of 18 and 19 December. However, as the paratroops had no working W/T sets and had moved their position to avoid detection by US troops, their requirements and their location had to be estimated, and the flights – which were carried out at the expense of interrupted supply operations to garrisons still holding out in the so-called Atlantic fortresses – were therefore largely unsuccessful.

The operation effectively came to an end on the 19th when von der Heydte decided to return to the German lines, and at midday on the 20th, he ordered his men to split up into small parties and make their way back as best they could. About a third of his men succeeded, but von der Heydte, who had jumped despite still recovering from a broken arm, was by now completely mentally and physically exhausted and he gave himself up to US troops during this withdrawal stage.

Even if the execution of the operation had been more successful, the *Fallschirmjäger* would, in any event, have remained isolated in enemy territory as the advance of 6. SS *Panzer* Army was delayed. Paradoxically, however, as the drop had been so widely dispersed, the Americans concluded that far more German paratroops were involved than was in fact the case, and the confusion caused behind the US lines was out of all proportion to the number of *Fallschirmjäger* actually involved.

By the 24th, the Ardennes offensive had ground to a halt due to fuel shortages and stiffening opposition as Allied forces were brought forward to strengthen the lines, and by 16 January 1945, almost all the ground taken by the Germans had been recaptured. The parachute operation proved to be the last undertaken by the *Luftwaffe*.

While TGr 30 continued air supply operations to the Atlantic fortresses, 3./TGr 30 was detached from the rest of the *Gruppe* in late March 1945, and transferred to Rheinsehlen where it was reinforced by II./KG 4. Operating together, the two units were known as *Einsatzgruppe* 'Uhl', named after the commanding officer, *Major* Fritz Uhl. *Einsatzgruppe* 'Uhl' was then joined by II./TG 3 and the two *Gruppen* worked together to supply *Feldmarschall* Walter Model's Army Group B which, following another of the *Führer*'s orders to stand fast, had become surrounded in the Ruhr on 1 April. Enquiries ruled out the possibility of air supply on an adequate scale but showed that Army Group B could expect 32 tons daily.

Supplies to Army Group B were so vitally needed that, in view of the lack of adequate landing grounds, Model suggested the use of seaplanes which could land on reservoirs. He also urged *OKW* to mount operations even if the aircraft were endangered, and indeed, great risks were taken when crews attempted to land on a series of hastily prepared strips. Most of these strips, however, were totally lacking adequate navigational equipment and had to be abandoned. Instead, aircraft released their cargoes over a series of dropping zones in the Wuppertal-Deilinghofen area.

Because of the difficulties, air supply remained on a minor scale and involved only 43 Ju 52/3m sorties and 18 flown by He 111s. The total of supplies delivered amounted to just under 100 tons, some 76 tons of which was rifle and machine pistol ammunition. Aircraft losses amounted to 11 Ju 52/3ms and four He 111s. Needless to say, the air supply sorties failed to meet the needs of Army Group B and the Ruhr pocket collapsed on 18 April. An interesting feature of the operation, however, was that the bases used, Ludwigslust and Werder, had previously been employed only for the air supply of the Russian Front. This was, therefore, the first instance in which air transport units supplied the Eastern and Western Fronts simultaneously from the same bases.

Air Transport on the Eastern Front
Summer 1944 to May 1945

In the summer of 1944, the *Wehrmacht* in Russia was overextended and its ground forces were holding a vast 1,400 mile front with few reserves. A Soviet summer offensive had long been anticipated, but when this began as a series of staggered blows in various sectors under the code-name *'Bagration'*, German forces were so stretched they were powerless to prevent major breakthroughs. The main attack opened on 23 June, with three Soviet fronts attacking Army Group Centre. Whole German divisions were annihilated and in two months the Soviets succeeded in advancing more than 700 kilometres.

In the north, the Soviets reached the Gulf of Riga at Tuckum on 27 July and isolated *Heeresgruppe Nord* in Estonia. They were unable to take the city of Riga itself, however, and the *Luftwaffe* attempted to fly provisions into the area. This operation took place in August and was conducted by II./TG 2 and

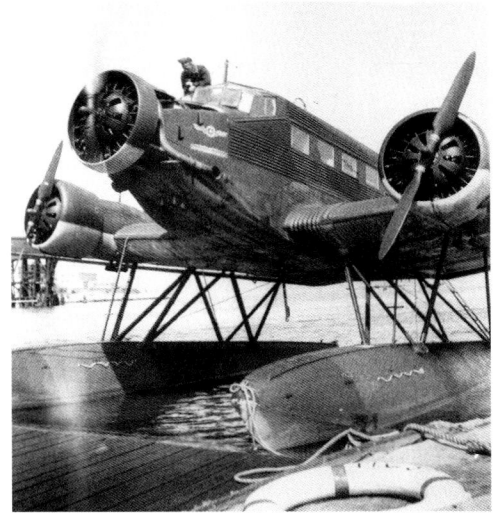

ABOVE LEFT AND RIGHT: A Ju 52/3m floatplane, almost certainly of TGr 20 in Norway, where the main purpose of the Gruppe was to convey urgent stores, such as aircraft spares, to points as far north as Billefjord. In the latter months of 1944, operations by this Gruppe were so severely restricted by a lack of fuel that it suffered long periods of inactivity. In a little-known incident on 25 October 1944, aircraft of the 2. Staffel were due to make a temporary transfer from Trondheim-Hommelvik to a destination in the far north of Norway in order to assist in the evacuation of key personnel and important material threatened by the Soviet advance. Take-off was delayed owing to bad weather, but as their aircraft had been fully fuelled and made ready, the pilot and W/T operator of the Ju 52/3m floatplane 7U+IK took advantage of the opportunity to desert to the Allies. After taking off, they headed north-west in the hope of reaching Iceland but encountered poor weather and bad visibility until, eventually, a shortage of petrol forced them to come down in a rough sea. They were later picked up by a fishing trawler and learned with surprise they were far south of their planned route and had come down 48 kilometres off the east coast of Scotland, near Aberdeen.

l./TG 3 under *Luftflotte* 6. The aircraft were based at Insterburg and brought out wounded on their return flights. These efforts, however, were to no avail and when German forces began to evacuate the area by sea in October, Riga fell to Soviet forces on the 15th. Elsewhere, the Soviets crossed the Norwegian frontier, and before Kirkenes was captured on the 25th, eight Ju 52/3m floatplanes of 2./TGr 20 were employed to fly key German personnel to the Oslo area.

Meanwhile, the Soviet Army's progress in the extreme south, near the Black Sea, was delayed until 20 August. On that date, attacking Soviet forces advanced through German and Rumanian forces, and Rumania surrendered on the 23rd. A ceasefire declared between Rumanian and German troops on 22 August was quickly broken and Rumanian forces opened hostilities against *Wehrmacht* units attempting to seize control and occupy Bucharest. The Germans, however, were greatly outnumbered and Hitler ordered in more troops to address the imbalance. The first of these were flown in by

RIGHT: When Rumania changed sides in August 1944, the giant Me 323s proved useful in transporting troops into areas of the country which were to be defended and also evacuating pockets of trapped German soldiers and considerable numbers of female auxiliaries. These operations were costly, however, and it is believed that by the end of the month between 12 and 15 Me 323s had been shot down or forced down by Rumanian pilots and anti-aircraft fire.

Ju 52/3m transports on the morning of the 24th to secure the airfields at Otopeni and Boteni near Bucharest, while further troops were landed at Tandarei in south-east Rumania. Details are scarce, but it is thought that one Ju-52/3m and one Me 323 which tried to land at Otopeni were hit by anti-aircraft fire and all the military personnel aboard were captured.

Following Rumania's declaration of war on Germany on 25 August, the bulk of German air transport traffic moved west and south-westwards to airfields in Hungary and Yugoslavia, and activity on the airfields at Budapest and Belgrade was markedly increased as numerous sorties were flown to extract German servicemen and women who would otherwise have been trapped and fallen into Soviet hands. During these operations, either flying in reinforcements to hold perimeters or to ferrying personnel out of danger, possibly as many as 15 Me 323s were lost as a result of the initial confusion caused by the Rumanian defection. On the evening of 25 August, one of these machines landed near the town of Alba-Iulia in northern Rumania, where the crew were taken prisoner, and another Me 323 which set out to rescue them crashed while landing. Four Me 323s were shot down on the 26th, and in separate incidents on the 27th, three more Me 323s were forced down. Two of these machines were obviously transporting troops for, apart from the crews, 147 soldiers were taken prisoner.

Meanwhile, the fuel shortage which affected units in the West in the summer of 1944, together with the need to draw on *Luftwaffe* personnel to replace infantry losses, also had a similar effect in the East as less economical units were disbanded. TG 5 was dissolved in August although it still had 54 Me 323s, some of which were assigned to IV./TG 4 which gave up its LeO 451s and also gradually took over the remaining aircraft of *Transport Staffeln* 4 and 5. Eventually, when the aircraft discarded in this reshuffle had been parked on various airfields and left to rot away, the only remaining *Luftwaffe* heavy transport unit was the *Grossraumtransportstaffel*, equipped with Ju 352s. Next to be discarded was IV./TG 3 which was disbanded in September, followed by the *Geschwader Stab* and the entire II. and III./TG 1, most of LLG 1, and what remained of LLG 2. Some crews and the powered aircraft of the *Luftlandegeschwader* were used to reinforce short-range reconnaissance units in the Balkans, but surplus gliders were stored where they happened to be and were not used again until the spring of 1945, when the Russian advances necessitated putting into the air every airworthy transport aircraft and glider.

TOP AND ABOVE: After the fall of France in June 1940, a large part of the country remained unoccupied by the Germans until November 1942. Known as Vichy France, the area cooperated closely with the Germans and retained an air arm which included a number of units equipped with the LeO 451 bomber. However, following the Allied landings in North Africa in November 1942, Hitler ordered Vichy France to be occupied and all French aircraft were seized. The Luftwaffe then began converting LeO 451s to transport aircraft and the type was later employed by KGzbV 2, KGrzbV 700 and TG 4, in addition to at least one independent Transport Staffel. This example, shown in France in Luftwaffe markings, was probably being converted to the transport role when photographed.

At the same time, since production of the last main batch of Ju 52/3ms had ceased in July, with the last 13 machines being delivered over the following three months, workshops soon ran short of spares and large-scale refitting was no longer possible. To offset this, all Ju 52/3ms remaining with *Lufthansa* and communications units were finally withdrawn while some He 111 *Kampfgeschwader* on the Russian Front began operating entirely in the transport role. Replacements for these Heinkel units and the existing TGr 30 were obtained from other bomber *Gruppen* as they were dissolved, or by calling on He 111s in the schools.

As Operation *'Bagration'* had pushed out a large salient to the north of Army Group South Ukraine, there was now a danger that this Army Group might lose contact with other formations on the Eastern Front and that Army Groups E and F might be isolated in Greece and Yugoslavia. Although Hitler delayed reaching a decision, he did eventually order a withdrawal, and despite the presence of Soviet forces in Rumania and Bulgaria, Army Groups E and F were able to retreat and join up with Army Group South Ukraine holding new defence lines in northern Yugoslavia.

During October, the Soviets overran the larger part of Hungary and by 9 November had advanced to the outskirts of Budapest, completing the isolation of the city on 27 December. Two days later, an air operation organised by *Generalleutnant* Gerhard Conrad of *Luftflotte* 4 began to supply the garrison's 70,000 German and Hungarian troops under *SS-Obergruppenführer* Karl Pfeffer-Wildenbruch, the commander of the IX. *SS Gebirgskorps*. The Ju 52/3m units employed were based at Papa and Szombathely in western Hungary and comprised III./TG 2 with 5./TG 2 attached and III./TG 3 with elements of I./TG 3 attached. There was also a Hungarian Ju 52/3m unit with a mere nine aircraft, and the He 111s of I. and III./KG 4, based at Wiener-Neustadt in Austria and Nowy Dwor in north-east Poland. Also available were the Do 17s and DFS 230 gliders of *Schleppgruppe* 2, but these were of limited value as most operations were to be flown at night and in bad weather, for which the standard towing method by means of a 40 metre long cable could not be employed. The alternative was to use a two metre long rigid tow bar to connect the glider to the towing aircraft, but the unit's Do 17s were not equipped for this. Some of the aircraft of III./KG 4 were suitably equipped, however, and some of the *Gruppe's* crews were experienced in towing techniques; as soon as they had completed their daylight operations, these aircraft and the appropriate crews were assigned to *Schleppgruppe* 2 for supply sorties.

Eighty tons of supplies per day were demanded, but as the requirements of the civilian population of Budapest could not be considered due to limited airfield capacity, most deliveries were to consist of ammunition, petrol, food, medical supplies and flour for the encircled troops. Twenty tons were to be air-dropped, and the remaining 60 tons of the total requirement were to be landed, with wounded comprising the load for the return flights. Various airfields were used as bases during the attempted supply of Budapest, but it was clear that the situation was hopeless and that such an operation would consume a substantial part of the remaining fuel stocks. Moreover, air transport capacity was inadequate and, although there were airfields inside the city, they were under artillery fire, with Soviet troops so close they were within grenade-throwing distance. Although Soviet fighter activity was slight, US fighters were very active and almost all operations were flown under cover of darkness. However, Soviet anti-aircraft and searchlight batteries proved a constant threat, and once an aircraft was caught in the beams of enemy searchlights, even the most skilled pilots rarely escaped. Additionally, the weather was usually bad with the constant danger of icing, and clouds of smoke over the city made identification of the drop zones difficult.

BELOW: SS-Obergruppen-führer Karl Pfeffer-Wildenbruch, the commander of the IX. SS Gebirgskorps in Budapest. Captured when the city fell, Pfeffer-Wildenbruch was taken prisoner but survived Soviet captivity and later returned to Germany.

ABOVE: In mid-December 1944, the Soviets advanced on Budapest and completed the encirclement of the city on 27 December. Two days later, responsibility for the air supply of Budapest was assigned to Generalleutnant Conrad, the commander of Luftflotte 4, and the first air supply operation was flown on the same day.

RIGHT: German troops preparing to board a Ju 52/3m after further reinforcements were ordered to the Budapest front in an attempt to relieve the city. When supply flights to the city began, 64 serviceable Ju 52/3ms were available, but when the operation came to an end six weeks later, more than half of these had been destroyed.

At first, aircraft carrying supplies were able to land inside the city, but on 9 January, the last airfield had to be given up and all loads were dropped by parachute. Supplies consisted mainly of ammunition, clothes and rations, but most of the containers released over the city by Ju 52/3ms were blown into Soviet-held areas. The He 111s were more successful in ensuring that supplies were delivered into German rather than Soviet hands, as crews of these aircraft employed a modified bombing technique. However, as the search for the containers could not begin until morning, it was often found that the contents had by then been stolen by civilians. An attempt to improve the accuracy of the Ju 52/3m drops by illuminating the target area was defeated when fuel in the city ran out, a factor which also further prevented the proper distribution of those supplies found and recovered intact.

ABOVE: The Hungarian Air Force received ten Ju 52/3ms, of which this is an example. Nine of these aircraft remained during the air supply of Budapest but proved of little use as they were invariably assigned other tasks by the Hungarian command staff.

Although the Hungarian Ju 52/3ms alone had been given the task of flying in 70 tons of ammunition and almost 350 tons of foodstuffs, this was a quite impossible target and, in any case, these aircraft were frequently away fulfilling some special operation at the request of the Hungarian command staff. Even the *Luftwaffe* Ju 52/3m units could only manage 36 tons daily, less than half the amount required to defend the city or even hold it for any length of time.

The contents of the supply containers delivered sometimes proved surprising. Some contained yellow flags to mark unexploded ordnance, while others contained Iron Crosses which were to be awarded to the defenders; when *SS-Obergruppenführer* Pfeffer-Wildenbruch was awarded the Knight's Cross for his part in the defence of the city, three had to be dropped before one finally reached him [4]. Other containers also contained items not required. On 29 January, the day before what was normally a German national holiday to celebrate Hitler's accession to power, special containers donated by *Reichsführer-SS* Heinrich Himmler and marked *'Spende Himmler'* [5] were dropped. When the containers were opened, they were found to contain sweets, cigarettes and tins of horsemeat, whereas hundreds of horses in the pocket were being shot and eaten daily as there was no fodder for them. The next day, *Oberst* Ernst Jansa, the commander of a Flak regiment in the city, acting in the name of the encircled troops, who most urgently required ammunition and flour, submitted a formal protest over the contents of the containers.

BELOW: Gliders were employed during the supply of Budapest when it became impossible for powered transports to land. Twelve DFS 230 gliders were destroyed during the operation and another 36 landed supplies inside the city but, as they could not be recovered, were also lost. These examples were photographed on Vermezo Meadow, one of the few emergency landing areas created in the city, where they had to be abandoned.

The last sorties in the operation to supply Budapest itself were flown on 9 February, and at 16.53 hrs on 12 February 1945, radio communication with the target area was lost. Later, it was learned that some 16,000 Germans had tried to break out and some 3,000 of these troops, located in woods by reconnaissance aircraft, were supplied by a small force of nine He 111s and three Ju 52/3ms during the night of 14/15 February. These were the last supply operations flown on behalf of the defenders of Budapest, and after the 16th, the Budapest garrison, which had regularly featured in the *Wehrmacht* daily bulletins, was not mentioned again. Of the troops who had broken out, only some 700 reached the German lines.

Not including the supplies delivered by KG 4, which was only occasionally available due to its commitments in the bombing role, a total of some 1,500 tons of supplies was delivered to Budapest, an average of 36 tons per day. Aircraft losses amounted to 36 Ju 52/3ms, more than half the original number employed, seven He 111s, one Ju 87 and 48 gliders. These losses were particularly hard to bear since they further reduced the already inadequate air transport capacity.

---

4. Pfeffer-Wildenbruch was also awarded the Oak Leaves for his defence of Budapest. Taken prisoner when the city fell, he was one of the last German PoWs to be released from Soviet captivity in 1956.
5. 'Donation Himmler'. In some accounts it is stated that the full wording on the containers read, 'Sonderspende, Tag der Machtergreifung', denoting a special delivery to mark the day the Nazis seized power on 30 January 1933.

At the beginning of 1945, the air transport forces underwent a fundamental reorganisation. On 10 February, the staff of the *Lufttransportchefs der Werhmacht beim OKL* was established and placed under the command of *Generalmajor* Friedrich-Wilhelm Morzik. This staff took over the functions of XIV. *Fliegerkorps* and the *General der Transportflieger* and, although this reorganisation came too late to be of any great benefit, the entire air transport system was at last placed under the control of a single staff. Its main tasks were to ensure that the little remaining air transport capacity was assigned to the various *Luftflotten* profitably, and that air supply tasks were carried out according to the urgency of military requirements and as effectively as circumstances allowed.

During the last few months of the war, the only transport units still available for operations were six Ju 52/3m *Transportgruppen*, one of He 111s, two He 111 *Kampfgruppen* on transport duties and one long-range air transport *Staffel* with Ju 352s (See also the table on page 168). Yet still these units struggled to bring what they could to the many surrounded localities and garrisons which were ordered to become fortresses and hold out to the last man. At Posen in western Poland, where 12,000 men were surrounded, 257 tons of supplies were flown in from 26 January to 23 February when the city was finally captured. Similarly, Schneidemühl, encircled on 1 February, was supplied from the 2nd by transports which flew in with 257 tons of supplies and took off with 277 people, 237 of them wounded. Breslau was encircled on the 16th and Grudziadz in Lithuania on the 20th. Also requiring supplies in February were Arnswalde, the encircled garrison in that part of Küstrin situated on the east bank of the Oder, and later Königsberg, which was outflanked on the 20th.

Transport Units available on the Eastern Front, early 1945

Unit	Aircraft	Kommandeur	Location
I./TG 1	Ju 52/3m	*Major* Oskar Schmidt	Tutow
II./TG 2	Ju 52/3m	*Major* Kurt Harnisch	Senftenberg
III/TG 2	Ju 52/3m	*Major* Gerhard Dudeck, later	
		Hptm. Hans-Hermann Ellerbrook	Dresden-Klotsche
I./TG 3	Ju 52/3m	*Hptm.* Georg-Dieter Matschullat	Senftenberg
II./TG 3	Ju 52/3m	*Major* Otto Baumann	Werder
III./TG 3	Ju 52/3m	*Major* Josef Penkert	Finsterwalde
Schleppgruppe 1	Do 17 towing DFS 230	*Hptm* Kurt Herzog	Königgrätz
	He 111 towing Go 242		
I./KG 4	He 111	*Hptm.* Rolf Rannermann	Königgrätz
III./KG 4	He 111	*Major* Herbert von Kruska	Königgrätz
Grossraumtransportstaffel	Ju 352		Tutow

Fortresses Requiring Supplies in 1945

(This table shows the sequence and duration of some of the more important supply operations)

Posen	26 January to approx. 23 February
Schneidemühl	2 to 13 February
Küstrin	2 February
Arnswalde	9 to 15 February
Glogau	17 February to 1 April
Breslau	15 February to 2 May
Gruzdziai	20 February to 4 May

As with supply operations in the West, sorties to supply the various fortresses on the Eastern Front could only be carried out at night. If possible, Ju 52/3ms landed to unload and bring out wounded, otherwise flights were restricted to supply drops. As a general rule, only ammunition was carried to the garrisons, but in some instances *Fallschirmjäger* and infantry were landed as reinforcements.

At the beginning of February, while some of these supply operations were still in progress, a determined effort was made to evacuate by air all unnecessary *Luftwaffe* personnel from the forward areas in East Prussia. After about 16 March, Königsberg was supplied by the Ju 352s of the *Grossraumtransportstaffel*, based at Tutow, which had been formed in January 1945 from parts of 13. and 15./TG 4. The majority of the weekly loads consisted of some eight tons of component parts for shells and other munitions which, after delivery to a landing strip south of Pillau, were assembled in the Königsberg arsenal. On the 23rd, Hitler ordered that all possible measures were to be taken to continue the supply of Fortress Königsberg, but on the same day *OKL* reported that it was doing all in its power to provide the necessary aircraft fuel, without which the fortress could not be supplied, and warned of a serious shortage on all fronts. After 3 April, only the fortresses at Breslau and Königsberg remained in German hands.

While exhausted and poorly-equipped German troops in the East fought stubbornly for every inch until overrun by the enemy, in the West, Allied fighters and fighter-bombers dominated the skies and prevented almost all movement by road and rail, at least by day, thereby increasing the workload placed upon transport units. Apart from poor weather, the lack of thorough training and combat experience prevented many of the transport crews from fulfilling the demands made of them. As a result, crash landings and technical failures took a heavy toll of men and aircraft, further reducing the transport units' capabilities. In these final weeks of the war, the continuing fuel shortage reached such critical proportions that before each operation, requisitions had to be submitted for approval by *Generalfeldmarschall* Wilhelm Keitel, who administered the so-called '*Führer* Reserves'.

In spite of all these difficulties, higher authorities refused to acknowledge that circumstances alone often prevented operational orders from being carried out and that many operations stood no chance of success. Unfounded allegations of cowardice in the face of the enemy and dereliction of duty were commonplace, and in such cases the responsible unit commanders were subject to trial before a military court for allegedly failing to obey orders. Fortunately, the investigating court committees consisted of experienced unit commanders who appreciated the true position and their findings invariably indicated that no one person could be held responsible for the alleged failure. Needless to say, however, such depressing investigations did nothing to increase the degree of operational readiness among the units, nor raise the morale of the crews or affect the degree of personal responsibility already felt.

Yet another burden was the vast number of reports which had to be prepared on the utilisation of remaining transport capacity. As the military situation worsened, Hitler granted special powers to various high-ranking individuals and staffs and ordered them to report to him personally on the conduct of operations. As standard daily reports were already being prepared for the appropriate *Luftflotte* and Army Group, as well as a number of unimportant Party and civilian agencies, they eventually became so numerous that operations were seriously hindered. Moreover, competition between the various staffs and individuals, all of whom wanted to demonstrate their efficiency by being the first to report to *OKW*, often resulted in the submission of incomplete and inaccurate information which only led to confusion and yet another investigation. Such a situation had arisen during the Budapest operation when, in an attempt to clarify the situation, Berlin demanded that details of take-off times and numbers of aircraft participating were to be transmitted direct in uncoded text. In order to maintain security, however, the Operations Staff had no alternative but to submit deliberately false and misleading information, so that eventually yet another senior officer arrived to check on the situation.

LEFT AND FAR LEFT: The useful load of a Ju 52/3m was up to 2,000 kgs. Here, Panzerfäuste and small arms ammunition are being carried aboard a Ju 52/3m where (*LEFT*) a Luftwaffe Oberfeldwebel stacks the Panzerfaust containers inside the fuselage. Note the machine gun mounted to fire through the fuselage window in the photograph (*FAR LEFT*).

When Breslau was encircled on 14 February, the Soviets intended to occupy rather than bypass the city, which became the focal point of a large-scale battle. The air supply of Breslau, which received top priority, began on the night of 14/15 February 1945, but the Soviets, realising that regular air supply would maintain the fighting capacity of the defenders, established strong anti-aircraft defences around Gandau airfield, directly east of the city. Additional searchlight batteries and guns of all calibres were moved into position so that no matter how the transport pilots approached, they were soon caught in the cross-beams of some 30 searchlights and came under concentrated fire. All manner of approaches were tried, from hedge-hopping to high altitude, and some pilots, hoping to avoid alerting the anti-aircraft gunners, throttled their engines to idle and silently glided down to land in the darkness. Nor was the danger over once the transport aircraft landed, for the Soviets were only half a mile from the airfield boundary and the unloading of supplies and the loading of wounded for the return flight had to be carried out under constant enemy bombardment. In addition to some 1,800 tons of supplies, most of which was ammunition, troop reinforcements were also flown into Breslau. Between 22 and 25 February, a *Bataillon* of *Fallschirmjäger* from the 9. *Fallschirmjäger Division* was flown into the city, and on the 26th Hitler ordered in another *Bataillon* which began arriving in the first week of March.

Since the Soviets might at any moment overrun Gandau airfield, work began on 7 March to broaden Breslau's Kaiserstrasse. In the event, the Ju 52/3ms were unable to use it, as an almost constant pall of smoke from the many fires burning in the city made night landings impossible. In late February, however, even before the work was finished, the Kaiserstrasse was used by DFS 230 and Go 242 gliders which, due to the shortage of transport aircraft, had been withdrawn from the stocks that had accumulated when the two *Luftlandegeschwader* had been disbanded in the previous summer. Towed to the target area by He 111s, the gliders were released at between 2,000 and 2,200 metres and silently glided down amid the dazzling glare of the searchlights and the flashes of gunfire and exploding shells.

These hazardous sorties taxed the endurance of the glider and transport pilots to the utmost, and although the glider pilots especially showed remarkable skill and determination in successfully completing flights to the fortress, the air supply of Breslau was not without its court investigations. All military authority had been transferred to the *Gauleiter* of the city, *SS-Obergruppenführer* Karl Hanke, who evidently failed to appreciate the limitations of air transport. Investigations following his constant radio complaints and distortions to Martin Bormann, the *Führer's* private secretary in Berlin, added a further burden to the already overworked air transport staff who were endeavouring to cope with the increasing organisational chaos of the last few weeks of the war. Typically, on one occasion, 28 heavy field guns were to be flown in, a task which would have required 240 sorties and consumed 480 tons of aviation fuel. After the weapons were dismantled in standard fashion, it was discovered they still would not fit into the Ju 52/3ms and that further dismantling was required by highly specialised personnel who were not readily available. However, in the time pending their arrival, it was discovered that the encircled force already had 50 of the same guns and that what it really required was ammunition for them.

The last transport aircraft to land in the city were three Ju 52/3ms which flew in supplies on the night of 6/7 April and took off with 52 wounded and two extra aircrew. Thereafter, supply drops were made, but when the airfields south of Berlin fell into Soviet hands, further supply flights became almost impossible. One of the lesser known units participating in the operation was *Transportgruppe* 'Herzog', a special ad hoc unit formed from 14.(*Eis*)/KG 55, parts of TG 3 and *Schleppgruppe* 1 and equipped with He 111s, Ju 52/3ms and Go 242 gliders. Also called in were the Ju 87 Ds of the night ground attack unit 3./NSG 4, with half of the participating aircraft dropping bombs while the other half released their supplies. On the night of 6/7 April, six of the *Staffel's* aircraft dropped eight containers with over two tons of ammunition to the hard-pressed defenders, but the missions were on too small a scale to have any significant effect and, indeed, cost the life of the *Staffelkapitän*, *Oblt.* Schmidt-Halfen on the following night. Even the fighter unit III./JG 53 dropped containers of ammunition and on 12 April, three light howitzers and a field cannon were dismantled and delivered by 16 of the *Gruppe's* Bf 109s.

Ultimately, some 1,000 Ju 52/3m and 2,200 He 111 sorties were mounted to Breslau in which an estimated total of between 2,600 and 3,000 tons of cargo was delivered. The last supply drops were made on the night of 1/2 May when seven Ju 52/3ms dropped supplies and two Fi 156s landed to pick up some glider crews. After that, supplies and aviation fuel simply ran out.

On the morning of 4 May, a delegation of Breslau's clergy called on the military commander and urged that the city be surrendered. Two days later, a representative met with his Soviet counterpart and offered to surrender on condition that the safety of the garrison was honoured. When the guns fell silent that night, 30,000 of Breslau's inhabitants, about a quarter of the population, had been killed, and as a direct result of enemy action, technical failure or weather-induced crashes, 165 transport aircraft, mainly Ju 52/3ms, of which 52 were aircraft from II./TG 3 alone, had been lost. *Gauleiter* Hanke fled the city in a Fieseler *Storch* but was later captured near Pilsen in Czechoslovakia [6]. Needless to say, the Soviets broke their pledge concerning the safety of the remaining inhabitants and subjected them to shameful excesses.

The Ju 52/3m could be fitted with a rack under the centre section to carry various containers. Once released, the container descended by parachute and the shock of the landing was absorbed by a concertina device mounted on the nose, as seen in the foreground of this view of an arms container being loaded.

---

6. Hanke was held in Czechoslovakia where he was later shot dead while attempting to escape. Following the revelation that Himmler had been attempting to negotiate a surrender with the Western Allies, Hitler had earlier appointed Hanke to the position of Reichsführer-SS.

RIGHT: Fw. Wilhelm Messer was awarded the German Cross in Gold on 28 January 1943 while serving with 15./KGzbV 1. Later, on 12 March 1945, when a Leutnant flying with 11./TG 2, he was awarded the Ritterkreuz and thus became the last of the Transportflieger to receive this decoration. Both decorations may be seen in this photograph as well as the Frontflugspange für Transportflieger above his left breast pocket. Given the timing of the award of the Ritterkreuz, it seems likely that this was in respect of the supply flights to Budapest.

Meanwhile, after a major offensive into Germany in January, Soviet forces had advanced to the Oder and were within 65 kilometres of Berlin and 160 kilometres of Dresden. During this advance, pockets of German resistance had again been bypassed to be dealt with later, but some small groups succeeded in making their way westwards. One of these consisted of troops from *General* Walther Nehring's XXIV. *Panzer Korps*, known as *Gruppe 'Nehring'*. As this *Gruppe* made its way north-westwards through Poland, it was supplied by air from the night of 16/17 January, mainly with tank ammunition and fuel in supply containers dropped by He 111s.

Eventually, on 22 January, after 11 days of fierce battles and night marches in which *Gruppe 'Nehring'* covered more than 240 kilometres, it reached the comparative safety of the Warthe river near Sieradz and made contact with *General* Dietrich von Saucken's *'Grossdeutschland' Panzer Korps*, which had been holding a line awaiting its arrival. Both formations then retreated westwards, and on the night of the 29th, 24 Ju 52/3ms succeeded in landing close to *Gruppe 'Nehring'* where they unloaded 48,000 litres of fuel and evacuated 206 wounded. Subsequently, both combat groups succeeded in reaching the west bank of the Oder near Glogau. Later, when Glogau itself became surrounded on 11 February, 21 Ju 52/3m and 237 He 111 sorties were flown between 17 February and 24 March in which 288 tons of supplies, mostly ammunition, were delivered for the loss of five aircraft.

LEFT: Lt. Fritz Kolb of 5./TG 3 was awarded the Knight's Cross on 9 June 1944. This photograph, taken on the day the award was presented, shows the long length of ribbon on which the medal was suspended for the investiture. The Ritterkreuz was worn in this way for one day only, after which the ribbon was cut to length so that only a short strip showed from beneath the collar and it was usually fastened around the neck by a piece of elastic or string. The surplus ribbon was saved in the presentation case and could be used to cut replacements as the original became soiled.

RIGHT: Ofw. Erich Jaschinski, who was awarded the Knight's Cross on 9 February 1945 while serving with I./TG 3.

LEFT: Another member of TG 3 to receive the Ritterkreuz on 9 June 1944 was Ofw. Karl Kern of the 6. Staffel.

RIGHT: An Me 323 of 6./TG 5 showing the gust lock in place on the tail control surfaces and what seems to be a tactical marking on the rudder in the form of a dark spot. Note the heavy exhaust staining over the wings and, just visible on the forward fuselage, the badge of II./TG 5. This Gruppe was disbanded in August 1944 and its remaining aircraft allocated to TG 4.

RIGHT: The Ar 232 entered service on the Eastern Front in early 1944 and was employed almost immediately on various special operations. In August a machine from I./KG 200 landed behind enemy lines in the Ukraine to rescue troops encircled during the Soviet advances and, despite heavy enemy fire, took off with 23 troops on board and returned safely at low level. A less successful operation was mounted to land saboteurs who were to destroy strategically important targets in the Moscow area, but the aircraft crashed near the city when it hit a tree and caught fire. This photograph shows one of the aircraft of TG 4 involved in an operation mounted under cover of darkness on 14 October to rescue troops trapped behind Soviet lines, which returned safely to Königsberg in East Prussia.

LEFT AND BELOW: Less fortunate was this machine which crashed into a parked Ju 88 night fighter while landing at Königsberg after the rescue operation. This aircraft, another Ar 232 A of I./TG 4, is believed to be W.Nr. 100008, coded G6+VY.

ABOVE: This Ar 232 is believed to be L5+DR of the Ergänzungs Transport Geschwader, the badge of which is on the aircraft's nose, although when this unit was disbanded in 1944, surviving aircraft were passed on to other formations. It is therefore possible that this photograph shows the machine while with another unit, possibly TG 5.

BELOW: This aircraft is believed to be the Ar 232 B-09, W.Nr. 110031. It is shown here when coded G6+UY of 14./TG 4, but when this unit disbanded the machine was assigned to 2./KG 200 and re-coded A3+SB. It was still serving with 2./KG 200 when it was shot down by a night fighter on 25 April 1945.

RIGHT: An SM.81 of Transport-gruppe 10 after being struck by a Luftwaffe Bf 109 G. This Gruppe was formed in early 1944 by redesignating an Italian unit first raised from personnel of the Aeronautica Nazionale Repubblicana, the Fascist air force formed after Italy capitulated to the Allies in September 1943. The Gruppe was employed only briefly in the summer of 1944 and was disbanded in October.

BELOW: This SM.82 belonged to TGr. 110, another transport unit manned with Italian personnel. The Germans, however, regarded the Italians as more of a liability than an asset and TGr. 110 was disbanded in late October 1944. This is one of their aircraft, later found in Germany by US forces. Although carrying standard Luftwaffe national insignia, the stylised green, red and white flag emblem of the Repubblica Sociale Italiana may be seen near the cockpit. When the Allies reached Celle airfield, they found another 21 of these aircraft, almost certainly of III./TG 1, completely burned out.

ABOVE: The interior of a Ju 52/3m loaded with ammunition. In the last six months of the war, when numerous cities in the path of the Soviet advances were surrounded and ordered to turn themselves into fortresses, most of these localities and garrisons soon ran short of ammunition and called for urgent replenishment by air. However, such operations were restricted by a shortage of fuel and the extraordinarily strong Soviet anti-aircraft defences.

ABOVE: Joachim Cöler was born in Posen on 1 June 1891. He joined the navy as an officer candidate in 1913 and was still serving with the Reichsmarine when he was accepted for flying training in 1915. His connection with naval aviation was preserved during and after the First World War, and, indeed, after he transferred to the new Luftwaffe. In 1940, he became commander of 9. Fliegerdivision and received the Ritterkreuz on 12 July. From October 1940 to December 1942, Cöler was commander of IX. Fliegerkorps and from 30 April 1943 commander of XIV. Fliegerkorps. He subsequently became the General der Transportflieger on 29 August 1944. He remained in this position until 4 February 1945 when his office was disbanded and he was replaced by Generalmajor Friedrich-Wilhelm Morzik. General a.D. Cöler survived the war and died aged 63 in Garmisch-Partenkirchen in May 1955.

RIGHT: When the larger part of TG 1 was disbanded in September 1944, only the I. Gruppe remained. All Staffeln of the Gruppe were equipped with the Ju 52/3m, but only the 4. Staffel operated the floatplane version. This example was photographed at Pütnitz in Pomerania in April 1945.

The Battle for Berlin

Before the Soviet advance to the Oder, Hitler had insisted that, for political and psychological reasons, any obvious defensive measures to protect the capital should not take place. It was, therefore, only on 14 January that *OKW* gave authority to issue directives concerning fortifications and defensive preparations to the east of the city. By early March, *Generalleutnant* Hellmuth Reymann, a *Luftwaffe* general, had been appointed commander of the Berlin Defence Area, and on the 9th he signed an order instructing that the capital was to be another fortress and was to be defended with fanatical determination, even down to the last hedge and shell crater.

By mid-March, the important airports at Gatow and Tempelhof had already been subjected to regular Soviet bombing, and on the 23rd, fearing that their continued use could not be assured, *Reichsminister* Joseph Goebbels, in his capacity as *Gauleiter* of Berlin, put forward the suggestion that the trees on either side of the Charlottenburger Chaussee, the broad, straight road running east to west from the Victory Column to the Brandenburg Gate, and also known as the East-West Axis, should be cut down in order to clear a landing strip. At that time, however, Hitler was still not convinced that Berlin would be the scene of the decisive battle and rejected the idea.

On 17 March*, Generalleutnant* Reymann held a conference in which the possibility of supplying Berlin by air was discussed. Unfortunately, displaying an unrealistic attitude typical of many of the higher German staff during the final days, and without any thought of the critical shortage of fuel and restricted capacity, Reymann demanded a daily delivery of 500 tons of supplies. To meet this demand, however, 250 Ju 52/3ms and 1,000 tons of fuel would have been required each day, yet at this time only 250 Ju 52/3ms remained and the daily fuel allocation for the entire *Luftwaffe* was a mere 800 tons.

The Soviet assault on Berlin began before dawn on 16 April, when three fronts with 19 armies, four tank armies, and three air armies, a total of almost two and a half million men, launched a huge attack preceded by an unprecedented artillery barrage. For two days bitter resistance restricted the enemy's progress to small bridgeheads, but by 20 April the Soviets had broken through the German lines north of Küstrin on the west bank of the Oder.

Two days later, during a dramatic conference on 22 April, Hitler learned that a trusted *SS-Obergruppenführer* had failed to carry out an important counter-attack. Flying into a bitter rage, he declared the war was lost but resolved to stay in Berlin where he would remain to the end and kill himself before the Soviets could take him prisoner. Although he quickly recovered his composure, he had come to the realisation that he would be unable to secure a military victory. What mattered now was to prolong the war until a split occurred between the Anglo-Americans and the Soviets so that some political agreement could be arranged. To that end, Hitler decided he would stay in the capital to command the forces assembled for its defence.

On 23 April, Hitler finally authorised the immediate construction of the proposed landing strip on the East-West Axis, and with great haste, trees and street lamps lining each side of the route were cut down in anticipation of large numbers of aircraft landing there. Meanwhile, an attempt was made from north-west Germany to fly in supplies and equipment. Particularly urgently required was ammunition, as dumps on the outskirts of the city had been overrun, but again, Army requests for air supply were unrealistic and proved impossible to satisfy.

BELOW: An example of the Ju 352. During the supply of Berlin in April 1945, the Ju 352s of the Grossraum-transportstaffel were able to land at Gatow until it fell into Soviet hands. The aircraft shown here was not an operational machine.

ABOVE: Soviet artillery in the streets of Berlin.

Taking part in the operation to Berlin were I./TG 1 and II./TG 3 with Ju 52/3ms, the He 111s of *Einsatzgruppe* Uhl (formed in March 1945 from 3./TGr 30 and II./TG 4 which were operating as a single *Gruppe*) together with the Ju 352s of the *Grossraumtransportstaffel*. By 25 April, two Soviet armies had encircled Berlin while the third advanced into the city itself. On the same day US and Soviet forces met at Torgau, thus effectively splitting Germany in two. Apart from Berlin itself, all that remained of the *Wehrmacht* in Germany were a few isolated remnants of Army Group Centre and Army Group Vistula.

In Berlin, the beleaguered city was now entirely dependent on air supplies, but although

ABOVE AND ABOVE RIGHT: The remains of one of two Ju 52/3ms which landed on the East-West Axis to deliver ammunition on the night of 26 April 1945 but which crashed while taking off loaded with wounded. It is thought both aircraft stalled while banking to avoid the Siegessäule.

surrounded by airfields, most had fallen during the Soviet encirclement and sorties were further restricted by the fuel situation. Only Tempelhof and Gatow airfields remained in German hands, and these were under increasingly heavy shelling. Yet despite this hopeless and critical situation, Hitler and his immediate circle in the *Führerbunker* continued their surreal, subterranean existence, making decisions about the deployment of forces so under-strength that they largely existed only on paper. In a world completely removed from reality, the mood alternated between despair and depression, and a tendency to view even minor successes with an unrealistic optimism. Indeed, as late as the night of 23/24 April, Hitler declared that the situation in Berlin was not really as bad as it appeared, and when it was announced that two Ju 52/3ms loaded with anti-tank ammunition had braved the intense Soviet artillery and mortar barrage and landed on the East-West Axis, it was as if a miracle had occurred and the news was greeted with outbursts of exuberance.

In the early hours of 26 April, three Ju 352s of the *Grossraumtransportstaffel* based at Tutow flew into Gatow with a battalion of marines under *KptLt*. Franz Kuhlmann of the *Kriegsmarine*, whose specific task was to defend the Reichs Chancellery and protect the *Führer*. Offloading the infantry of the *Marine-Bataillon* was accomplished quickly on account of the shelling, and within 20 minutes of landing the aircraft had been reloaded with wounded and all aircraft returned safely to Tutow. Less fortunate were the two Ju 52/3ms which had landed on the East-West Axis. For their return flights, each aircraft was again loaded with wounded, but both machines crashed while taking off.

LEFT: An Fi 156 abandoned at Berlin's Gatow airfield. Aircraft of this type were to fly a supply mission to Berlin on 27 April 1945, but although the machines were prepared and arrangements made to provide a fighter escort, the operation failed due to weather conditions and heavy anti-aircraft fire over the city.

On the following day, six Fi 156 aircraft which were supposed to fly to Berlin in the evening with an escort of 30 fighters were made ready at Rechlin. The operation failed, however, because the aircraft became scattered in heavy rain and most met heavy anti-aircraft fire which forced them to return damaged or to make emergency landings. Only one Fi 156 succeeded in reaching the correct area of the city but was unable to locate the East-West Axis because of the rain and a great deal of smoke.

At the military conference held in the *Führerbunker* on the night of the 27th, it was announced that 50 aircraft, each with one and a half tons of supplies, were expected to land that night. In the event, landing proved impossible, although some of these aircraft may have succeeded in releasing their loads in the vicinity of the East-West Axis as it was reported at the conference that air-drops had already commenced.

Luftwaffe Air Transport Order of Battle, 25 April 1945

OKL Gen. Qu.

Stab Lufttransport Chef d. Wehrmacht		Berchtesgaden	

Luftwaffenkommando Kurland

1./TG 1	Ju 52/3m	Windau	11

Luftwaffenkommando West

1. & 2./TGr 30	He 111 H–20	Neubiberg	16

Luftwaffenkommando 4

III./TG 3	Ju 52/3m	Wimsbach	37
Transport Staffel 200	Fw 200	Hörsching	2

Luftwaffe General Norwegen

TGr 20	Ju 52/3m	Oslo	38
See Trans. Staffel 2	Ju 52/3m W	Hommelvik	7

Luftflotte 6

Transport Staffel 40	Fa 223	Ainring	3
	Fl 282	Ainring	3

VIII. Fliegerkorps

Stab TFF (Luftflotte 6)	–	Prague	–
II./TG 2	Ju 52/3m	Schrasslavitz	32
III./TG 2	–	Klattau	–*
I./TG 3	Ju 52/3m	Neuenburg	24
Stab KG 4	He 111	Königgratz	1
I./KG 4	He 111	Königgratz	24
III. /KG 4	He 111	Königgratz	23
1./Schlepp Gr. 1	Ju 87	Königgratz	3
2./Schlepp Gr. 1	Do 17	Königgratz	11
	DFS 230	Königgratz	15
3./Schlepp Gr 1	He 111	Königgratz	15
	Go 242	Königgratz	6

Luftflotte Reich

Stab TFF Lft. Reich	–	Rerik	–
Stab and 2./TG 1	Ju 52/3m	Tutow	14
3./TG 1	Ju 52/3m W	Pütnitz	15
II./TG 3	Ju 52/3m	Güstrow	34
3./TGr 30 and Gruppe Uhl	He 111 H–20	Rerik	27
Grossraumtransportstaffel	Ju 352	Tutow	23
II./KG 4	He 111	Greifswald	28

* Aircraft given up to I./TG 3; dissolved 30 April 1945.

Other Ju 52/3ms were made ready to fly in *Waffen-SS* troops from Rechlin-Mecklenburg, but the airfields at Tempelhof and Gatow had fallen to the Soviets earlier that day and the Ju 52/3ms returned to Rechlin. Another attempt was then made by 12 Ju 52/3ms which were ordered to the East-West Axis, but landing again proved impossible due to concentrated anti-aircraft fire, the almost constant artillery barrage and shell craters. One aircraft which attempted a landing crashed on the East-West Axis, the crew of another spent an hour searching for the approach without success, and others returned damaged. The last flight out of Berlin was made on the 28th when the newly-promoted *Generalfeldmarschall* Robert *Ritter* von Greim, formerly C-in-C of *Luftflotte* 6, left the city with the aviatrix Hanna Reitsch in an Ar 96.

Further flights continued to release supply containers along the East-West Axis which bisected the area of continued resistance, in places now barely one and a half kilometres wide. Flying conditions were extremely difficult as, quite apart from strong opposition from concentrated anti-aircraft guns and Soviet fighters, Berlin seemed to be on fire everywhere, creating a dense mixture of dust, smoke and fog which hung over the city and sometimes reduced visibility to less than 50 metres. In the hope that smaller, faster types might be able to achieve what the slower transports could not, fighter and ground-attack aircraft also released supply containers, although few of these could be recovered.

The attempt to supply Berlin involved a total of about 200 transport flights, but although they helped to raise morale, they had no tangible value and resulted in the loss of between 20 to 30 transport aircraft. On the 29th, *General* Helmuth Weidling, the current commander of the Berlin defence area, reported that transport aircraft had dropped only a few tons of supplies during the night and that, as none were expected in the coming night, the city would run out of ammunition within the next 24 hours.

When *SS-Brigadeführer* Wilhelm Mohnke, the commander of the inner defensive zone of Berlin, confirmed that his forces were in the same plight, Hitler made his last decision, and in the afternoon of 30 April, he and the young woman he had married the night before, committed suicide. The Chancellery was finally stormed on the night of 1 May, and at first light on 2 May, *General* Weidling broadcast an order to all German troops to lay down their arms. Thus the city was surrendered, although it was another two days before the fighting died completely.

In one bizarre twist, Lt.-Gen. Peter Kosenko, Chief of Artillery in the Soviet 5th Shock Army, later reported that although aircraft had been seen taking off from the Charlottenburger Chaussee during the last few days, nobody could identify the type or say who were the passengers. He then went on to state that Hitler was certainly not in the Chancellery when his troops arrived, thus fuelling post-war speculation that the *Führer* had fled Berlin and was still at large. [7]

BELOW: Clouds of smoke rising from buildings destroyed in Berlin's Frankfurterallee on 2 May 1945, the day that General Helmuth Weidling surrendered the city to the Soviets. Frankfurterallee was close to Hitler's bunker and the emergency airstrip created on the East-West Axis.

ABOVE: One of the units which assisted in the attempts to supply Berlin was Schlachtgeschwader 10, under the command of the Ritterkreuzträger Major Helmut Viedebannt. He was killed near Wusterhausen-Dosse on 1 May 1945 when the parachute on the supply container he was carrying opened prematurely and his Fw 190 crashed. The city surrendered the following day.

BELOW: A Fieseler Storch in the Tiergarten in the centre of Berlin. In the background is the Siegessäule – the Victory Monument – which marked the eastern end of the emergency airstrip on the East-West Axis.

7. Typical of such accounts are claims that, after shaving off his moustache, Hitler had fled Berlin via an underground tunnel and boarded a Ju 52/3m floatplane which then took him on the first stage of a journey to Brazil, Argentina or elsewhere in South America.

Unconditional Surrender

With the fall of Berlin, it was generally anticipated in the West that a final collapse was now a matter of days, perhaps hours, away. Gradually, German government agencies, service channels and administrative arrangements had broken down under the cumulative weight of bombing and advances by enemy ground forces and only isolated and sporadic fighting continued. To all intents and purposes, the war on the Western Front was over and, as units surrendered in increasing numbers, the forces of the *Wehrmacht* rapidly disintegrated. As early as 1 or 2 May, a Ju 52/3m of TG 3 landed to surrender to US forces at Herzogenaurach, and on the 4th, the same day that German forces in Holland, north-west Germany and Denmark surrendered to the British 21st Army Group, the commanding officer of TGr 30 took it upon himself to permit his men the use of the remaining aircraft to take off for whatever destination they chose. Three men attempting to reach their homes near Nuremberg landed their Fieseler *Storch* in a field near Ansbach but were immediately apprehended by American troops, while another *Storch* landed at Straubing. More fortunate was the crew which crash-landed their He 111 in a field near Frankfurt-Höchst in the early morning of 9 May and quickly made off in civilian clothes. When American troops arrived to inspect the crash site, they found only the crew's uniforms inside the fuselage. By this time, formations in contact with the western Allies had been ordered to lay down their arms as the battle against the Western Powers had 'lost all meaning'. The final, official cessation of hostilities came into effect on 8 May when Germany surrendered unconditionally.

Summary

From the first extensive use of air transport in Norway in 1940 to the last day of the war, the transport units proved their value in carrying supplies of war materials and food to the Army forces in the field. On numerous fronts, in various theatres of war, and despite tremendously high losses, as summarised in the following tables, the *Transportflieger* continued to carry out daily sorties without adequate fighter cover. Some of these operations involved flying in supplies to ground forces retreating in the face of superior enemy formations, or to isolated pockets of resistance attempting to reach friendly territory. In either case, without the support of the *Transporters*, the troops would otherwise have faced almost certain annihilation. That these successes were possible is attributable to the astonishing reliability and long life of the Junkers Ju 52/3m and the overall dedication and unshakeable morale of the *Transportflieger*.

Table of losses 1939-1945

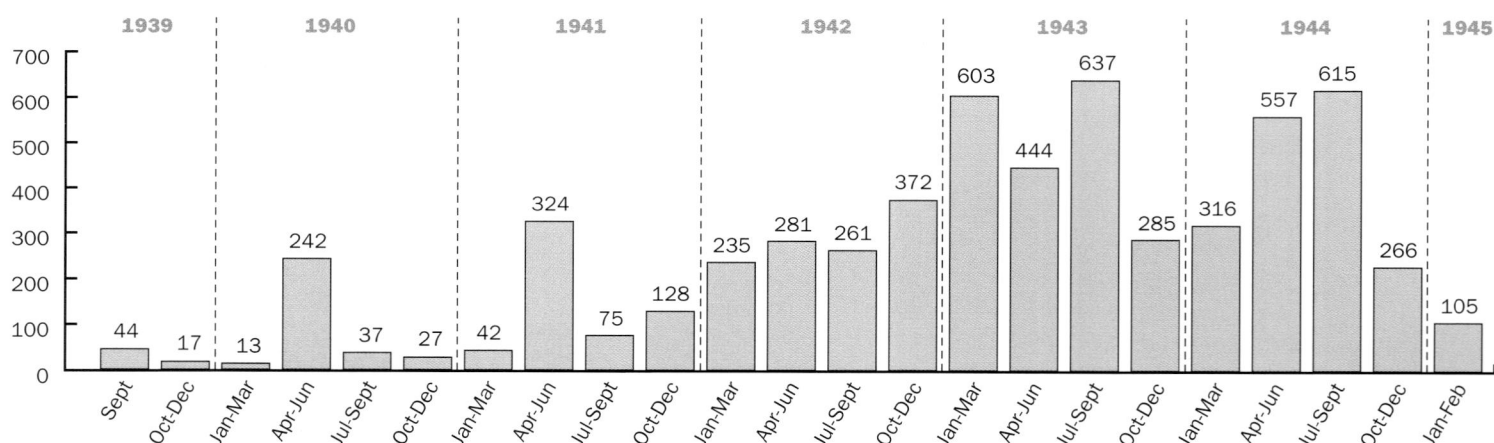

Normal Establishment of Air Transport Units, 1945

Stab Transport Geschwader	6 Officers, 44 NCOs and men	1 Communications Aircraft
Gruppenstab	7 Officers, 60 NCOs and men	1 Communications Aircraft
Transportstaffel	6 Officers, 121 NCOs and men	16 Transport Aircraft [i]
Seetransportstaffel	6 Officers, 121 NCOs and men	16 Transport Aircraft (Floats)
Ju 352 Transportstaffel	7 Officers, 116 NCOs and men	12 Ju 352
Me 323 Transportstaffel	3 Officers, 218 NCOs and men	12 Me 323 [ii]

i. TGr 30 was an exception. This Gruppe found that an establishment of 16 aircraft was unwieldy and in June 1944 reduced the number to ten.
ii. This establishment is purely theoretical as the Me 323 units had been dissolved by 1945.

RIGHT: An Fi 156 C-3/trop of TGr 30 which landed at Straubing in May 1945 where its occupants surrendered to US forces. The code S3+UA indicates that the aircraft belonged to the Gruppenstab, and all characters were in green, narrowly outlined in white. The W.Nr. 8138 appeared in white on the fin.

BELOW: US personnel examining the He 111 – almost certainly from TGr 30 – that crash-landed near Frankfurt-Höchst at about 05.00 hrs on 9 May. The crew had escaped wearing civilian clothes. An interesting feature was that the only operational marking was a white or yellow letter O aft of the fuselage Balkenkreuz.

LEFT: The personal marking on the rudder of this He 111 employed by TGr 30 shows a trailer with the legend, 'Wir transportieren alles!' – 'We transport everything!' – marked on the side.

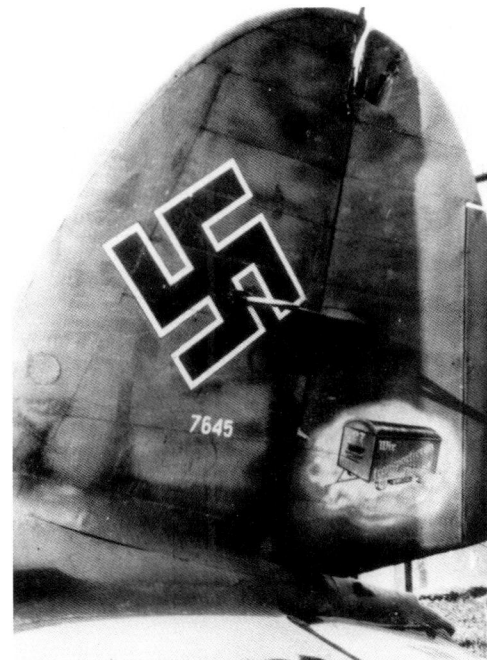

ABOVE: The tail of an He 111 H-20, W.Nr. 700628, at Schweinfurt in 1945 showing again the light blue 76 lines, typical of TGr 30, which were sprayed over the dark green finish to divide it into segments. This aircraft, coded S3+ML, had belonged to 3./TGr 30 but the whole tail unit was a replacement, as shown by the different camouflage on the fuselage and the aircraft letter K on the rudder.

1943-1945

LEFT AND BELOW: An He 111 H-20, W.Nr. 701412, of TGr 30 at Gross Ostheim, Germany, in February 1945. As this unit operated almost exclusively by night, the undersurface camouflage on this machine, which carried the operational code S3+HK, was black and the aircraft was equipped with flame dampers. The 70/71 uppersurface camouflage has been segmented with an elaborate overspray of RLM 76 which, given the time of the year, was an intelligent use of available paints and provided a finish suitable to blend with a light fall of snow.

BELOW: The fuselage of an He 111 of 2./TGr 30 found in Germany in 1945. The operational markings have been painted over an earlier code, possibly indicating that this machine was an H-16 transferred from KG 53. This may also account for the camouflage, which is slightly different from that normally employed by TGr 30.

ABOVE, ABOVE RIGHT AND RIGHT: This Ju 87 D-2, W.Nr. 412211, was photographed at Fritzlar in 1945. Coded 8M+EH with the 8M in small black characters, the aircraft had earlier belonged to 1.(DFS)/Schleppgruppe 3 and had been used to tow DFS 230 gliders. Since Schleppgruppe 3 was disbanded in September 1944, this aircraft was almost certainly transferred to 1./Schleppgruppe 1, a unit known to have had three Ju 87 Ds still on strength at the end of the war.

Junkers Ju 87 D-2 of 1./Schleppgruppe 1, Fritzlar, Germany, May 1945

Still wearing the operational code 8M+EH of 1.(DFS)/Schleppgruppe 3 from which it was transferred, this aircraft of 1./Schleppgruppe 1 had faded RLM 70 and 71 uppersurfaces and RLM 76 undersurfaces. A spiral was painted on the tip of the spinner and the aircraft letter E was narrowly edged in white. Although ostensibly a glider tug, the flame dampers over the exhausts and the bomb racks retained under the wings suggest that aircraft may have found additional employment in the night harassment role. The W.Nr. 412211 appeared at the top of the fin in white.

ABOVE AND ABOVE RIGHT: This He 111 H-6 of 4./TGr 30 landed at Mönchengladbach on 6 May 1945, when the crew and passengers surrendered to US forces. The machine was finished in a conventional 70/71/65 camouflage but with the Staffel letter 'M' in the operational markings S3+EM finished in blue, the Staffel colour, whereas the normal practice was to paint the aircraft letter in the Staffel colour.

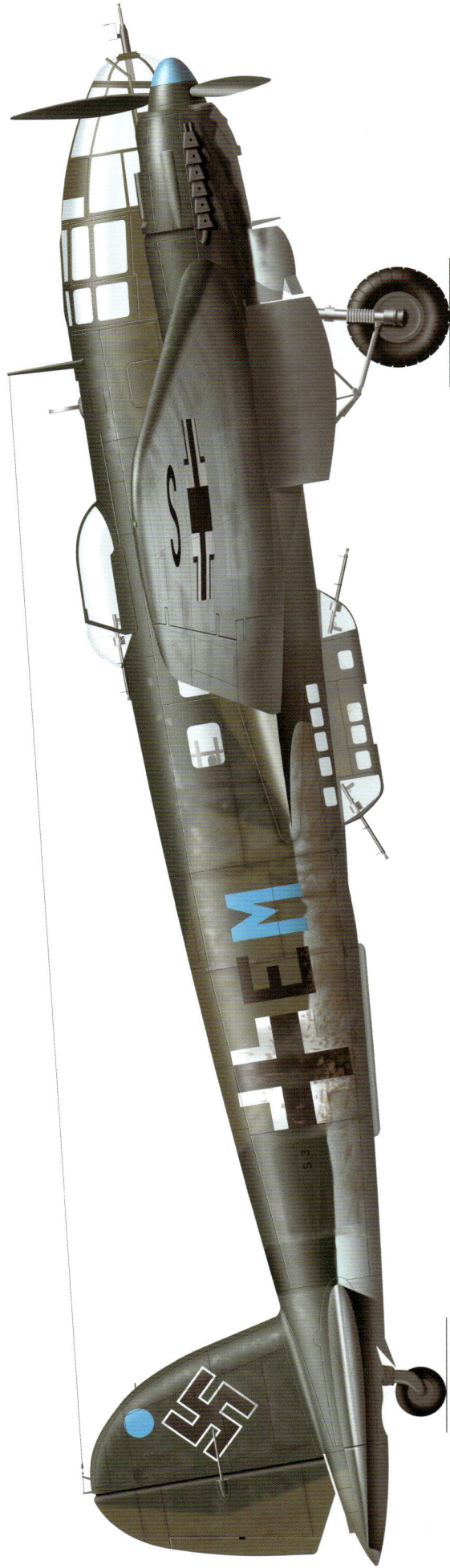

Heinkel He 111 S3+EM of 4./TG 30, May 1945

This aircraft had evidently flown previously with different operational markings as areas of fresh paint on the fuselage showed where an earlier code had been overpainted. Similar overpainting had also occurred on the fuselage band, where the top half had been obliterated, and the change of aircraft identity may explain why only the first and last characters of the code S3+EM had yet been applied under the wings. Note the tactical marking in the form of a blue disc on each side of the fin.

ABOVE AND BELOW: Two views of an He 111 H-20 which was found at Berlin-Gatow after the surrender in 1945. The machine, which had flown transport missions with 8./KG 4, carried the operational code 5J+ES with the E in red narrowly edged in white. The rear parts of the spinners were also in red, the Staffel colour, and the undersides of the engine cowlings were yellow. Interestingly, while the undersurfaces remained in standard 65, most of the original green 70 and 71 on the uppersurfaces had been oversprayed with what is believed to have been 81, over which are large sprayed patches of 76. Note, however, that the 70 and 71 splinter pattern is still visible towards the top of the fuselage and that the swastika has been partly obscured by the revised colours. The rudder, but not the trim tab, is evidently a replacement with darker patches of fresh colour.

1943-1945

THIS PAGE AND OPPOSITE: This Ju 52/3m, carrying the operational code 4V+MV of 11./TG 3, was photographed after landing at Herzogenaurach where its crew surrendered to US forces on 1 or 2 May 1945. Note in particular the very worn and faded appearance of this machine and the repainted areas on the fin, rudder and fuselage where the tactical and operational codes have been changed.